*This Book is Dedicated to the*
*Healing of Nations and World Peace*

Supreme Science Qigong Center was founded in 1999 and became Press on Qi Productions in the year 2008. Back in our early days, we created 100's of seminars with many respected veteran Qigong Practitioners from all over the world. Many years later a great dream was realized. We gave the Qigong away for practically nothing!! And what happened? The good people showed up in massive gatherings to practice Qigong under one roof. As of 2010 we've certified over 1000 highly trained Qigong Instructors and they spread the knowledge to many. We believe the power of these Qigong Healing techniques can transform the world. In light of such aspirations, we formed a 501c-3 Non-Profit Organization called Supreme Science Qigong Foundation, for whose mission is to bring REAL Qigong to the masses of people at the lowest possible cost. The time for empowerment is now.

*Special thanks to audio genius: Jami Deva for playing the best music at every Qigong Workshop.*
*Special thanks to video/production genius: Anthony Wallen & Lew Aronoff*
*Special thanks to musical talent: Paul Horn, David Helpling, Jon Jenkins, Marconi Union & Kamal*
*Special thanks to everyone else that made the vision real: Kai VBS, David Beaudry, Dietrie & Norwood Yamini, Patricia Pollari, Steve Wood, Kelly Perko, Darla Reynolds, Sheila Janan, Jocelyn Brock,, Paula Branton, Vito DeMalteris, Hanna Lose-Frahn, Tommy Dale, Roger Aguiar MA, Renee Speir, Paul Dong, Weizhao Wu, Tom Wu, Wim Hof, Professor Tanya, the other 975 instructors, my parents, my children and most of all God.*

*This information is not meant to treat, prevent, or cure any disease and is not endorsed by the FDA.
*Please share this information with your health care provider before making any changes to your diet.
*Please know that we have taken pain staking measures to verify the accuracy of these writings to the very best of our ability.
*Photocopying and Plagiarizing is prohibited. Written permission can be obtained to reference for true educational purposes.

These Qigong exercises are copyrighted by Press on Qi Productions Inc. Only certified instructors from SSQF with signed certificates may duplicate or teach these exercises to the public. Please obtain proper training first before teaching. Animations and keywords such as 'Press on Qi' & 'Press on the Edge of the Energy Field' are trademarked and considered intellectual property under international law. Methods taught within this training are not meant to replace a physicians instructions. These teachings are not meant to diagnose, prevent or cure any disease. For more details visit www.QIGONG.com

# Table of Contents
## Qi Revolution ~ The Training Begins
### Level 1 - Level 2 - Level-3

Qigong for Life

Natural Medicine

# Saturday Level-1

## Qi Revolution: The Training Begins

**"The men of old breathed clear down to their heels."**
*- Chang Tzu, 300BC*

9:00 AM - Introduction to Qigong: The 3 Types of Energy & The True Source
How Qigong Accomplishes Healing
Ancient Chinese History & The Nature of Qi Energy

9:45 AM - The Breath: Key to the Energy Kingdom
Mechanics of the Qigong Breath — Feeling Qi Exercise

10:00 AM - Empty Force - Qigong Exercise #1
Ready Position and Opening Procedure
Spiraling, Pulsing and Pressing on Qi: Subtle Movements
Gracefulness: The secret power behind Qigong and the SSQ "Fog Theory"

Short Break

11:00 AM - Breath Empowerment: Initiation to "Activate & Clear Energy Body
Group Sharing of Experiences

12:30 PM - Lunch Break (90 minutes)

2:00 PM - Level-1 ANIMATED Qigong Healing Routine
*Empty Force - - - - - - - - Qigong Exercise #1
*Cloud Hands - - - - - - - -Qigong Exercise #2
*Earth Hands - - - - - - - - Qigong Exercise #3
*Around The World - - - Qigong Exercise #4
*Push Hands - - - - - - - - Qigong Exercise #5

Question & Answer Session
Short Break

3:30 PM - DEEPER PRACTICE with Jeff: Level-1 Qigong Healing Form
*Taoist Stretching:    Isometrics and Creating your Own Push-Pull Resistance
*Hamstrings, Quadriceps, Gluts (Easy & Moderate Versions)
*Abdomen, Back, Shoulders and "Shake It" to close

Short Break

5:00 PM - Keynote Presentation #1: Food-Based Healing Science "Conquering ANY Disease"

# Sunday Level-1

## Qi Revolution: The Training Continues

**"Holding on to negative emotions is like grasping hot coals.
You are the one who gets burned."** *-Buddha*

**9:00 AM -** Opening Prayer to Source
Food-Healing Demonstration
Smoothie Tasting followed by Questions about Food Healing

Short Break

**11:00 AM -** Instructors Take the Stage
Level-1 Qigong Healing Form

Short Break

**12:30 PM -** Qigong Walking Group Practice (Spiral Formation)
    \*Breathing and Walking Simultaneously
    \*Holding & Spiraling the Qi
    \*Bone Marrow Washing
    \*Concealed Qigong Walking

*Seamlessly woven into...*

Internal Qigong Meditation "Full Body Breathing"
Using the Qigong Heart/Mind
Harmonizing the 5 Yin and 5 Yang Organs

**1:30 PM -** Lunch Break  (90 minutes)  *GET YOUR SAMPLE SMOOTHIE OUTSIDE!*

**3:00 PM -** Taoist Five Element Theory  *With Preview of Shake It Exercise*
Physiology and Human Behavior

Short Break

**3:30 PM -** Advanced Discussion and Instructor Demonstration of Level-2 Form
    \*Full-Body Cleansing:  Rooting, Qi Follows Mind & Practicing with Spiritual Heart
    \*Drawing the Bow:  Shifting Weight, Push Movements & Projection Movements
    \*Full-Body Spiraling:  Using Minute Spirals to Draw Energy into Pituitary Gland

**5:00 PM -** Animated Energy Practice:  Level-2 Advanced Qigong Form  *(minus Nine-Breath Method)*

Short Break

**6:00 PM -** Keynote Presentation #2:  Origin of the Universe, Prosperity Consciousness & Miracles

# Monday Level-2
## Qi Revolution: The Training Climaxes

*"Health is the greatest possession. Non-being is the greatest joy.*
*Do the difficult things while they are still easy." - Lao Tzu*

9:00 AM - Opening Prayer to Source
Keynote Presentation #3: The Other Side
   *What happens when people die?  What DO we know for sure?
   *The Power of Prayer to MANIFEST your Life's Highest Possibility  (Amazing!!)

Short Break

11:00 AM - Taoist Stretching:  Mental Preparation for Deeper Level of Practice
Deeper into Level-2 Advanced Qigong Form  *(minus Nine-Breath Method)*
   *Full-Body Cleansing
   *Drawing the Bow
   *Full-Body Spiraling

Short Break

11:45 AM - The Ultimate Qigong Breathing Practice:  Nine-Breath Method Seated Practice
   *Precautions about this Exercise
   *9 Warrior Breaths
   *Breath Lock and Sink Down
   *Nine-Breath Method:  TUMO VERSION A

Short Break

1:00PM - Nine-Breath Method:  TUMO VERSION  B
   *Total Comprehension of Version A & B
   *Overview of 9-Breath Healing Circle

Short Break

2:00PM - 9-Breath Hands on Healing
      *Laying on of Hands
      *Miraculous Qi and Universal Qi
      *9-Breath Qi Transmission:  Sending Qi Knowing All is One

3:00PM - Lunch Break  (90 minutes)

4:30PM - Nine Breath Method Healing Circle
The Ultimate Group Energy:  *For healing self, loved ones and our planet!*
Live Music Acts and possible celebration beyond words

# Tuesday Level-3

## Qi Revolution: Advanced Training Complete

*"Seek and you will find; knock and the door will be opened to you." - Jesus*

9:00 AM - Opening Prayer to Source
Intense Energy: Back to Back Level-1 & Level-2 Forms
Closing Nine-Breath Connection to Mother Earth

Short Break

12:00 PM - Introduction to Wuji Style Qigong: Level-3 Formless Form
Keys to Creating Beautiful/Powerful Wuji
Learn the 7 Broad Categories of SSQ Wuji Style Movements
Animated Presentations of Each Movement

Short Break

1:00 PM - Practice Level-3 Wuji Formless Form

1) Subtle Movements: Spiraling, Rotating, & Spiral-Rotate Simultaneously
2) Ball Making Movements: Open-Close Style & Palm-Facing-Palm
3) Push Hands Movements: Moving Body with Force-of-Energy
4) Projection & Drawing Movements: Pointing the Arrow & Receiving
5) Locomotive Movements: Counter Rotating Horizontal & Vertical
6) Cleansing Style Movements: Washing and Brushing
7) Swimming Style Movements: Pressing on Qi with Entire Body

2:00 PM - Lunch Break (90 minutes)

3:30 PM - Keynote Presentation #4: Sacred Geometry, Secret Wonders and Humanity's Future

Short Break

5:00 PM - Advanced 9-Breath Method Meditation   TUMO VERSION C & D
*Prolonged Retention
*Prolonged Sublimation
*Adding Additional Warrior Breaths
*Global Healing Meditation (Advanced 9-Breath Method Series)

Short Break

6:45 PM - GLOBAL HEALING MEDITATION using Advanced 9-Breath Method

# Introduction

## *Theory & Understanding of Qigong*

# How does Qigong Heal?

*- Explaining why Qigong does what no other form of exercise can do.*

*Over 4000 years ago Chinese medicine said, "Blood is the mother of Qi".*
*The old testament Leviticus 17:11, "For the life of the flesh is in the Blood."*

During Qigong practice we feel a powerful pulsation of blood in our body. Often it takes people by surprise how warm they feel after making just a few hand movements. Qigong moves a lot of blood and generates a lot of energy without lots of movement or stress.

Often people ask "What is a Qi blockage?" It is simply a small area where the blood cannot go, or an area where disease can occur. For example, some people may have a knot in their stomach or bad digestion. Qigong usually improves this condition. *Blood can work itself through closed off capillaries when a person is relaxed and increasing Qi in that area.* Wherever Qi goes, blood follows. Normal healthy people use about 60% of the circulatory system. When our Qi increases this percentage is also goes up. Blood flow to the brain and organs is improved, therefore our health is greatly benefited. The electrical aspect of Qigong also plays a role. More on that later.

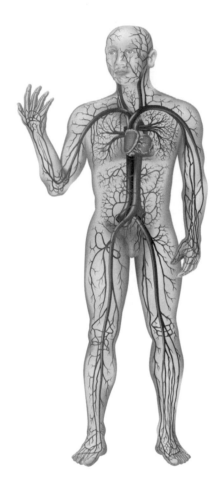

So how is this any different than jogging? In Qigong the body is totally relaxed, yet the blood is mobilized to flow powerfully. Because there is no stress response or cortisol release, which contracts blood vessels, the blood can enter areas that may have been blocked off for years. Microcirculation to the forehead is increased and digestion is greatly improved. **Imagine the same blood circulation you get from jogging—while standing still...completely relaxed.** No other exercise offers this level of circulation to organs and endocrine glands. Stiff shoulders beware... Qi and Blood coming through.

## Health Benefits and Effects of Qigong

Qigong has powerful health-promoting effects: (1) Improves the motion of blood, warms the blood and enhances whole body circulation. (2) Stimulates appetite, sexual function, assimilation of nutrients and digestion/elimination (3) Accelerates metabolism, weight loss, decreases need for sleep (4) Bolsters the immune system by reducing cortisol, a known inhibitor of cytokine production (5) Develops dexterity, reflexes, and prevents Osteoporosis in clinical studies (6) Opens arteries allowing greater brain-based microcirculation to prevent Alzheimer's disease (7) Enhances mental acuity, focus and concentration. The Qi draws focus and trains the mind. (8) Helps us to calm down, relax and become more peaceful. (9) Harnesses the power of True Source, remarkably improves results of hands on healing, such as Reiki, and helps spiritual growth.

# Healthcare Practitioners REALLY need Qigong

Healthcare practitioners can prevent themselves from getting drained by seeing lots of sick patients. This is a fact for many therapists and nurses that I encounter. Each year we train hundreds of registered nurses and nearly all of them complain that they constantly feel drained. Often massage therapists take on the aches and pains of their clients. While this may sound superstitious I assure you the phenomena is real. Often doctors who specialize in a certain aspect of medicine are exposed to a certain "Energy Information Signal" so frequently that they end up with the same problems they are surrounded by. *What is a healer supposed to do?* By using Qigong one can easily cleanse their energies. Dianne Dougherty is a nurse that we trained who says she is no longer effected by other peoples energy after learning Qigong. Now she has energy to finish her shifts. She is dedicated to a daily practice.

## Qigong in the Media

Oprah Winfrey's beloved Dr. Oz said on international television, "If you want to live to 100... do Qigong." He also said, "Qigong is the best longevity exercise". After this November 1st, 2007, show I feel it will be a short time before Qigong is embraced by the American mainstream audience. There are thousands of scientific studies that show Qigong has helped people to reverse cancer, diabetes and heart disease. If you want to read these scientific studies visit QigongInstitute.org where you can find the largest database of scientific papers on Qigong's effects.

## Why practicing in Groups is the KEY

Healing occurs in Qigong when one raises their energy high enough to push through the blockages of the nervous and circulatory system. Whatever Qi touches will be rejuvenated by it, however people are often blocked and thus need *stronger energy* to clear the pipes so Qi reach the problem areas. Some schools teach that people need the help of a powerful master to send strong energy for that initial boost. After personally training with 7 high level Qigong masters I do not believe this to be true. The most effective way to begin the healing process is to enter a large group energy field. They knew it China when they repeatedly gathered 30,000 at a time and people were getting up out of wheel chairs. I saw a retired nurse enter my seminar wheeling a walker. On the 4th day she was walking laps around the massive ballroom without her walker. In all honesty, the Qigong is very powerful, but it is the group energy that turns it into overdrive. Every person has a biological magnetic field. When a group of even 3 people practice together the results are at least double. A larger field is created than any of us could generate on our own in the big Qigong events. Being in this high amplitude energy is the single fastest way to jumpstart one's internal energy. This is the understatement of the century.

| • | • | •• • | • • • • • <br> • • • • • | |
|---|---|---|---|---|
| I Person Without Using Qigong & Prayer | I Person Actively Using Qigong & Prayer | 3 People Actively Using Qigong & Prayer | 10 People Actively Using Qigong & Prayer | 500 People Actively Using Qigong & Prayer |
| *5 Units of Energy* <br> *Present in the Room* | *25 Units of Energy* <br> *Present in the Room* | *150 Units of Energy* <br> *Present in the Room* | *700 Units of Energy* <br> *Present in the Room* | *100,000 Units of Energy* <br> *Present in the Room* |

# The True Source of ALL Things

*400 Billion Galaxies and The Universe still goes out farther than we can see...*

Since ancient times, man has marveled at the beauty and sheer size of our universe. Plato, Pythagoras, and Leonardo Di Vinci all realized that this universe required a master architect. How else could each snail have a perfect Fibonacci spiral the same as every galaxy? How else could your body function on so many deep chemical levels unless it was created by a master designer? We must understand that we are created by the Infinite Living Mind. Everything in creation starts with a point of origin. Without this reference point...one cannot fully awaken.

When learning about God we can see that many people have been lied to. *Many people have created human characteristics for the Infinite Living Mind.* THE ALL is beyond form and beyond what our minds are capable of understanding. What is able to be observed/studied are the universal laws the creator has laid out.

# Seeing the Bigger Picture of Qigong

Genesis Verse 1:1   In the beginning God created the heaven and the earth.
Genesis Verse 1:2   And the Earth was **WITHOUT FORM, and VOID.**
                    And darkness was on the face of the deep.
                    And the spirit of God moved upon the face of the waters
Genesis Verse 1:3   And God said let there be light: and there was light

God said let there be light! And so it was. 400 Billion Galaxies. Its doubtful that God had to "do" Qigong or some task to "create" the light. Most would agree that God probably "created the light with thought". So what does this mean? That we live in a Universe created by the "Mind of God". God is the "Infinite Living Mind" behind the creation. You are holding a manual reading these words. The paper... the particles... are all made of quarks and atoms... yet at its fundamental level... its most basic level... *This is a Universe created of thought.*

Qigong harnesses the energy pulsing through creation. For me, its the most powerful way to access my potential. To bring out the power of my SPIRIT. What is the human spirit? No one knows for sure. It can be moved and circulated within the body for healing. And at times... when conditions are just right... a miracle can happen where one is literally "overflowing" with the holy spirit. That level of Qigong is beyond technique. It is when the "blessing" lands on us. We can practice Qigong like a machine and generate lots of Qi. Still this would be limiting. The higher levels of Qigong begin when we practice with sincerity. Whereby each breath... and each move... becomes a sacred thank you.

# The Three Kinds of Energy

## - Understanding Qigong and the Supreme Science

1) <u>Internal Qi:</u>   Also known as Personal Qi.   This is the energy already inside of your body. It is the energy that beats your heart and keeps you vital.  The idea is to use Qigong to increase our internal energy, and thus improve health with Qigong.   Some methods work more with the energy already inside you, whereas other methods place more emphasis on absorbing External Qi.  Both methods are needed.

2) <u>External Qi:</u>   Also known as Surrounding Qi. All around us Qi is "alive" in the air we breathe. When practicing breathing techniques we are drawing on the External Energy around us and putting it inside our body... in effect making it Internalized. External Qi represents all the energy in the universe that is not currently inside your body. The movements of Qigong are passing through the energy ether that is all around us.  When we move slow enough we can feel it and harness its force to charge our body.

3) <u>Miraculous Qi:</u>   This energy has little to do with breathing techniques or special qigong moves. It is an intelligent energy that usually appears "without notice" and leaves an instant healing or sudden enlightenment in its wake.  It cannot be stored by the body as external Qi can. It usually stays for a few minutes only and then vanishes without a trace.  Miraculous Qi is well documented and appears to be intelligent running through a person's body giving them exactly what they need. This energy is the same "Holy Spirit" that has been landing on people during prayer for thousands of years.   It is impossible to use a technique to acquire it. Its the *divine blessing* and you'll never forget it as long as you live if you see it. Sometimes people in certain churches "shake" from the great power of this energy.  It is associated with prayer, being humble and reverent states of awe.

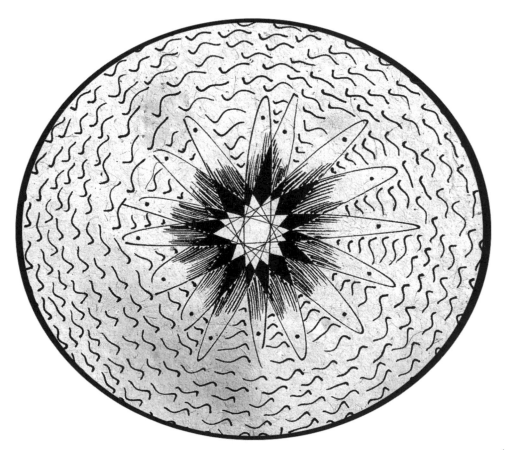

# The Day I Learned to Heal

*- How I came to the conclusions that I have*

A few years ago, my girlfriend at the time injured her knee in a ski accident. The ski patrol carried her on a snow mobile down the mountain; when I met her at the bottom, she looked in agony, "I need to go to the hospital!" she said. Her knee was swollen with visible internal bruising. It was a reasonable request. Even so, spirit moved me to insist she sleep first, before going to the hospital. The next morning, she woke up and sat up on the edge of the bed. When she tried to stand up, she winced horribly in pain. I asked her if she was willing to let me try Qi healing on her knee. She agreed, both reluctant and hopeful.

I practiced Qigong for an hour and returned to the room when my hands were fully charged with energy. But instead of my usual approach, I was guided to try something different. I stood beside the bed and asked her, *"Do you believe you can be healed, totally and completely, on this very day?"* She looked doubtful, but said "Yes." I placed my hands over her knee and began practicing my usual method of focused Qigong breathing. The pulsation between my hands and her knee became very intense; after 20 minutes, she said, "I can feel a strong current flowing from your palms." Sensing the opportunity I asked again: "Do you think it is possible to heal completely on this very day?" She smiled and her eyes filled with tears. "Yes," she said. "I do believe it is possible."

You probably know how the story ends. For 30 minutes I held my hands over her knee while doing concentrated breathing reciting a silent prayer. Suddenly, she heard a clicking sound and exclaimed, "I just heard my knee click!" I slowly pulled my hands away and asked her to try walking. She did, without pain. I then asked her to jump up and down! Tearful, she jumped repeatedly without pain. *In that moment I realized that something different had happened that I had never before seen.* Her knee looked normal without even so much as a bruise. She was totally healed.

# Energy Healing and Divine Blessing

*- Merging of the Eastern and Western Philosophies*

This type of miraculous healing is rare. Christianity refers to this energy as the "holy spirit". To create less conflict we call it the "miraculous Qi". Sometimes this miraculous Qi will "decide to land and heal the person". It may come...and it may not come. It has nothing to do with breathing or Qigong and its appearance can never be promised. Miraculous Qi runs under different laws than Universal Energy or Surrounding Qi. It appears to have a "mind of its own" and comes to people while praying. *Thus I am a big believer that people pray in addition to Qigong, however its not required. That is the whole point. Prayer is not required to get a good result with Qigong. Qigong works like a machine. Yet... the greatest healers throughout history have known that the "ultimate energy" comes from blessing and my own experience tells me it is the key.* Supreme Science Qigong understands that everyone has different beliefs and that these are sensitive issues. We could just "not mention" these phenomena to avoid problems, but I believe that most people (studies show 90%) do believe in God, the True Source, Tao or whatever you call the "Original Mind". We feel it is in your best interests to understand the difference between the body's physical Qi/universal energy with that of the divine blessing. We encourage you to practice with sincerity.

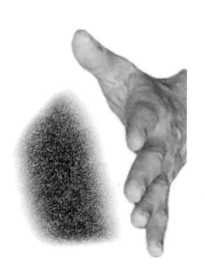

# What is Qigong?

1) Gathering and circulating internal energy with graceful movements

2) Using a multitude of breathing techniques to absorb Qi

3) Intelligent use Medicinal Plants and Qi-Rich Foods

4) Massage and acupressure practices for simulating meridians

5) Arranging environment to be in harmony with the natural flow of energy

6) Doing good deeds *(without telling others)* to obtain righteous Qi

# Ancient History

| Yellow Emperor's Birth | I-Ching Book of Changes | Lao Tzu & Confucius | Written Publication of | Chang San-feng. |
|---|---|---|---|---|
| *Gave his famous discourses on Longevity and Qi* | *Peng Tzu - Dao Yin Qigong* | *Tao Te Ching* | Yellow Emperor's Classic | Founder of Tai Chi Chuan |
| 2700 B.C. | 1800 B.C. | 600 B.C. | 300 B.C. | 1247-1358 A.D. |

In Taoist lore, Huang Ti *(the Yellow Emperor)* is the original creator of the longevity practices which Qigong has been linked to. The book "Yellow Emperor's Classic of Medicine" is the first written account of the concept of Qi. The book is so detailed and precise that it is still used in its original version throughout Oriental Medicine Colleges today. This book is a written account of the yellow emperor's conversations with his chief medical advisor, Chi Po. The time which the Yellow Emperor is believed to have lived and made his discoveries is 2700 B.C., however the book first appeared in written form around 300 B.C. If you desire to know Qigong's origins you should buy it. This book is very complex and the best translation is by Maoshing Ni, Ph.D.

*Dao-Yin Silk Scrolls Found inside tomb at Mawangdui, China 200 B.C.*

Peng Tzu *(pictured above)* is said to be the creator of Dao Yin. This is a method of moving Qi with long slow extensions of the limbs combined with deep abdominal breathing. Many regard him as the actual founder of Qigong, but really he took what was being practiced and advanced it. He is the most recognized of the "Taoist Immortals" and believed to reach 777 years of age.

Tai Chi is a much more recent creation. Qigong masters designed these long dances and movements originally to disguise Martial Arts practice. It has been proven to help seniors keep their balance and coordination as well as increase bone density. Tai Chi places emphasis on Alignment and Rotating from the waist. These rotating movements can resolve many common digestive problems.

# Chinese Medicine & The Three Treasures

The 3 treasures used in Chinese Medicine and Qigong are referring to alchemical components in the human body. As the *'building blocks of life'*, the three treasures need to be looked after, nourished, and developed. Each of them is interrelated and connected. Therefore, if one is out of alignment it effects the others. Three treasures is a way to identify 3 major causes of health problems. It takes many years of study to understand Chinese Medicine and this in no way can compare to being trained in Chinese Medicine. The explanations given below are designed to be simple and accurate reflections of how the ancient Chinese doctors looked at the human body-mind-spirit organism.

1) **Jing:** Sperm and Ovum are the most powerful examples of Jing in the universe. Any *secretion* from the body that produces 'energy' is considered Jing. Hormones, saliva, breast milk, and sexual fluids are good examples. These fluids are high in Qi and cannot be instantly replaced. Many times when a person has fatigue it is because their Jing is low. Male Sperm is by far the most concentrated source of Jing in a man's body. Frequent ejaculation will weaken any man with time. As for women, menstruation is the main cause of Jing loss, since the body brings all the best nutrition and Qi to the uterus in the hopes of creating new life. When this does not occur and the woman sloughs off the unused lining of the uterus, which is high Jing, a woman can feel emotional and low energy. The female deer exercise taught in Level-2 is a great way to temporarily halt or greatly reduce heaviness of menstruation. *The two best foods to increase Jing are Maca Root and Goji Berries.*

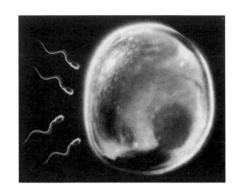

*The Human Body puts forth its best energies during the act of Procreation. All sexual fluids and hormones carry tremendous energy potential.*

2) **Qi:** Its the Electromagnetic Lifeforce which permeates every square inch of the universe. A wise man once said, "The Qi is in the Air". Therefore, breathing techniques are a key component of a successful Qigong wellness program. The body is constantly using hormones and nutrients (Jing) and transforming them into Qi (energy). Food becomes important when considering your Qi. Raw foods contain the pure Lifeforce energy of the sun and it is encouraged to eat a portion of your diet in a raw state in a smoothie. Also, the sun is pure Qi energy for healing! Yes, while its true that the sun can burn, the sun can heal you too. 30 minutes of sunlight daily is a great addition to your diet and will keep your energy high. *See Conquering ANY Disease manual for details about sunlight.*

3) **Shen:** It is said to be the energy of the Head. Its presence, or lack thereof, can be seen in the eyes. It is the *mental energy or will power*. It provides a person with focus, concentration, and creativity. Shen directly translated means 'spirit'. The spirit is "fed" by the Qi. Having more Qi connects you deeper with your spirit and is good for <u>all</u> spirituality.

## Three Aspects of Self

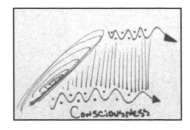

*We exist on 3 levels of being:*
*Our body is the form (Jing)*
*Our spirit is the energy (Qi)*
*Our mind is consciousness (Shen)*

*We can strengthen our physical form*
*We can strengthen our spiritual form*
*We can strengthen our mental form*

# The Nature of Qi is like Fog

According to the ancient Qigong Masters, Qi permeates every square inch of the universe. Unlike oxygen, Qi is everywhere, yet its nature is elusive. Everyone is receiving energy *all the time* from the True Source unconsciously. Qigong gracefully increases the amount we receive by using our intentional mind (meditation), our breathing, and our physical movements. When it comes to movement, in order for the Qi to be absorbed by the body, the Qi needs to be "embraced by graceful hands". One needs to understand the Nature of Qi.

Have you ever found a piece of dirt floating in your glass of water? If you try to grab the dirt out with your finger, the moment your finger touches the water it pushes the dirt out of the way. Even if you try to put your finger underneath the dirt, when it rises the force will push it out of the way. Therefore, sometimes it is difficult to take a very small bug or piece of dirt out from water. We could say that it is "elusive". The Qi is a lot like this in many ways. Imagine the Qi like a "Living Fog" that permeates your environment. If you move too abruptly, this pushes the fog away from you. If you move with fluidity and grace you can 'absorb' this fog in your hands. The "Fog Theory" helps you absorb more Qi. *You will notice that slower movements yield more pulsation of blood and a much stronger sense of the "electromagnetic energy field" during practice.* That is because you are gently touching the Qi without it being pushed away. It gets absorbed. Recall that according to Chinese medicine, "Wherever the Qi goes... blood will follow." **Graceful and precise movements will increase the healing effects of Qigong "Tenfold". Sudden or abrupt movements give a weak Qi feeling**. We strive to move slow and create an awareness of this energy that hangs like a living fog all around us. In such a fast-paced world it can take effort to consciously slow down and be more precise in our movement. We call this "Moving with Sincerity". It is a higher level understand-

Emanating from "The Source"
The Universal Qi Plasma Floats
Like a Fog and is easily Disrupted.

Grace is more than Cosmetic...
Abrupt Jerky Moves "Brush Away" Qi.
Steady Precise Movements are Required
For a Good Result in Qigong. Embrace the Qi.

# Ideal Practice Space and Feng Shui

Your living environment is one of the real keys to success with Qigong. Your practice space has tremendous impact on how deep your practice will be. Feng Shui is the now popular Oriental art of interior/exterior living arrangement. The ancient Qigong practitioners thousands of years ago observed that building the temple on the riverbank was favorable to the flow of abundant Qi. In contrast, they also observed that building near stagnant/still water areas was unfavorable to health. They could see that Qi was not abundant in these areas. Everyplace has Qi, but some more than others. Feng Shui supports health and spiritual growth.

Many schools of Feng Shui have emerged with complex systems to help you decide what color your bed sheets should be. They use 5 elements and try to harmonize yin and yang in the home/office. After years of studying Feng Shui we have determined it is a legitimate art form, however it is often unnecessarily complex. Real Feng Shui does

My first spiritual teacher was a shaman from Siberia. She had spent years living on a Taoist monastery and it clearly showed. Inside her house there was no furniture aside from 2 chairs in the far corner next to a small table for drinking tea! The house was empty with hardwood floors and it was the best Feng Shui possible. In her backyard there was even a forest! The energy of her house was alive—and empty!

Since the time of Buddha and Jesus masters have sought refuge in the Mountains. They knew a powerful secret! Mountains are powerful magnetic generators filled with minerals for conducting higher energy amplitudes. To increase your personal and spiritual power as well as 'recharge' there is no better place. Rivers carry the life force of the Earth and Waterfalls are teaming with natural healthy ozone and magnetism. Imagine sitting at the base of a 200 year old pine tree while doing 9-Breath Method! Finding the ideal spot to practice Qigong is also Feng Shui. I have "made friends with" a pine tree on the bay and have meditated under it for years, however I prefer to do standing Qigong forms in my studio on Tatami.

Below are the most important aspects to Feng Shui:

1) Keep your house clean. Free of dust and clutter.
2) Center of each room kept empty so Qi can accumulate.
3) Place all furniture on the border of the room.
4) Try to keep windows open whenever possible.
5) Mirrors in practice room amplify Qi and correct your form.
6) Minimize number of Do-hickys you own. Less is more.
7) Use wall space instead of floor space.

# Qigong Glossary of Terms

**Internal Qi**: The Lifeforce Energy that already exists inside you. Chinese medicine postulates that our kidneys and liver store Qi and that we have a "Qi Bank Account". The adrenal glands draw emergency Qi from the kidneys immediately upon being startled or put in a life or death situation. All people have internal Qi, but some have a lot more than others. It was taught to me by my teachers that when a person has low internal Qi they will get sick if the Qi is not replenished. The goal of Qigong is to increase internal Qi and therefore improve health and connection to

**External Qi**: The Lifeforce Energy that exists outside your body. It is the energy within the Air, Sunlight, and Food we eat. In Qigong we take the external Qi or environmental Qi and bring it inside our body. When we use the Nine-breath Method, our breathing takes in large amounts of external Qi. The Tumo breathing then circulates this external Qi and it is absorbed by the body organs and tissues. Once external Qi is absorbed it becomes internal Qi. Internal Qi is responsible for good health.

**Internal Qigong:** Meditation where one does not move the body is a "pure" Internal Style of Qigong.

**Internal Method:** Uses mental imagery or willpower to absorb and circulate energy through the body. *Visualization is the main component*. The Full-Body Cleansing is an example of an internal method since you to visualize white light moving down the front of your body. Most of the Qigong we teach has both internal and external methods combined. Visualizations are powerful. They set in motion bio-chemical processes with measurable by factors like heat and pulsation. *The Qi follows the mind*.

**External Qigong:** Any movement-based art like Tai Chi or Martial Arts where this is no mental component to guide energy or visualize is a "pure" External Style.

**External Method:** Nearly all Qigong taught by SSQC has both Internal and External methods combined. Movement-Based Qigong is the foundation of our system. Some schools of Qigong have a stronger emphasis on Internal methods such as mediation. We emphasize movement-based Qigong based on the notion that blood and Qi need to move in order to flow properly and avoid stagnation. The best external Qigong forms are combined with Visualization, Intentional movement of Qi and

**Hard Qigong:** Often used in martial arts. Empty Force is a an example of a 'light' Hard Qigong. Usually demands the student to stand firmly with arms held outward in particular Qigong postures.

**Hard Method:** Techniques that are physically demanding and increase muscular endurance are Hard. The premise of SSQC's Qigong is that it should make you physically stronger. Drawing the Bow in L-2 form uses a hard method by having you bend at the knees more to further lower your stance. This makes your legs strong and increases your internal Qi. We are all athletes. Hard methods can always be tempered when injury prevents the full participation. Most are surprised by their capabilities in the workshop. The Qi energy helps people in unknown ways to be stronger and have what it takes.

**Wuji Qigong**: Any Qigong that does not follow a set routine of movements or series of exercises. SSQC system of Wuji Qigong uses 7 Broad Classifications of movements that are used spontaneously.

**Wuji Method:** Spontaneously doing whatever movement or exercise feels right in that moment.

# The Qigong Breath: Long & Slow

The average person breathes 12-15 breaths per minute. Dogs frequently take up to 200 pants per minute! Tortoises on the other hand breath 1-2 times per minute. Who do you think is the smartest species? Many tortoises have been documented to reach over 160 years old, but there are legends of a special white tortoise that lived over 300 years old! Of course that is just a legend, but why did the ancient masters so revere the tortoise? It knows how to regulate its breathing. This is the key to its longevity.

# Qigong Breathing

The "Qigong Breath" is a relaxed form of breathing and should be used in your daily living and working states, not only during your Qigong practice.

Inhale: Bringing air in through your nose, inhale to **below** the abdomen. This form of breathing is known by many names: The Buddha's Breath, Baby's Breath, Fetus Breath, etc. Because it's the way that both babies and enlightened people breathe. This is the *most important* practice in Qigong and the mastering of this deep belly breathing is the mark of a master. As you advance, you will begin slowing the speed of your inhalation. The belly must literally come outward in order for this to work. See picture if unsure.

Exhale: While expelling air out 'sweep' your abdomen back towards your spine. This is a literal sweep as the abdomen physically moves **slowly inward**. This creates a strong Qi flow in your body every time you breath. It also massages your internal organs. The exhale is done only with your abdomen so don't think about your chest. Bring your mind to your naval and visualize your abdomen moves all the way inward. This is equally important to the inhalation since this action removes the toxins from your body.

# Breath Empowerment #1

When we are receiving the empowerment it is important to understand what is actually happening. This empowerment is not given by another person or master, but by your breath. Large amounts of Qi will enter your body and create a vibration. Some will feel this vibrating very powerfully like an engine and others will simply notice a slight tingling. It depends on your body constitution. I have only seen profoundly positive results emerge after taking over 20,000 people though it. There is an audio CD recently developed that allows people to experience the benefits at home.

# Feeling is Everything

Becoming sensitive to the Qi is important for success in Qigong. When you are able to feel lots of energy, it means you are connecting to the 'Sea of Qi' all around you. Feeling the Qi is also helpful for attaining transcendental states of consciousness. There are several Qi feelings to be aware of:

1) Heat in the Naval and Hands
2) Tingling/Vibration
3) Pulsation
4) Hands full of blood (Red Palm)
5) Magnetic Sensation

Qigong is really about feeling and not about empty movements. Some movements may look quite beautiful on the surface, but without a strong magnetic Qi field it is limited in its application. Therefore, you can be your own judge as to whether you are progressing well in your practice. Many people who practice Qigong already can dramatically improve their results by correcting their hand posture. The arms need to be rounded. Certain positions of the hands and arms are more conducive for attracting Qi. When the movements are performed smoothly you can 'collect' more Qi from the Sea of Qi all around.

The magnetic sensation is the most important with regards to external "movement based" Qigong. The best External Qigong styles will create a strong magnetic field in your hands. Other practices such as Pranayama Breathing produce more Vibratory sensations as does Qigong Meditation. When you feel this magnetic field getting stronger that means Qi is moving faster in your body. You will notice that the hands will pulsate much more powerfully when you are holding the Qi. Why? Because the Qi is in the blood. Therefore, tangible sensations of magnetism and pulsation will usually occur together.

# Empty Force Qigong

This system of Qigong was taught to us personally by Master Paul Dong. He did not invent the method himself, but he did master the process as he demonstrated quite clearly his ability to push people backwards from several feet away without touching. He is pictured here moving this woman through a door at my home in the Fall of 2001. How did he do it? Moving people is actually not very difficult and can be preformed by anyone who understands the magnetics behind our Push Hands exercise, which comes later on.

# Level-1 Workshop

*Qigong Healing & Breathing Applications*

# Introduction: Level-1 Qigong Healing Form

The hallmark of the Level-1 form and Supreme Science Qigong is using subtle movements and "Moving with Sincerity". This means that each move is gracefully executed and precise. This allows you to move effectively through the universal "Energy Plasma", which God generously gives to sustain life . *This plasma of energy around us is subtle and delicate.* Wind carries it back and forth in nature, yet it is better to practice without any wind. It is when the energy becomes almost still, like a calm perfectly still lake, that you can really feel its healing power tangibly like a thick substance. When you move slowly and with "sincerity" the energy plasma is undisturbed and is easily absorbed by your body. For this reason our styles move slower than most. We are perfecting movement. Often people who have taken Tai Chi-Qigong for 20 years or more will remark that after studying this particular form that they have a new-found sensitivity to Qi.

# The Fastest Way to Increase Muscular Endurance

### *- 30 Minutes of Supreme Quality Exercise*

There is an opening procedure, five primary exercises and a closing procedure. In total, the Level-1 Qigong Healing Form takes about 30 minutes and you will be standing on one spot for that time. Your body gains a different kind of strength than that gained by jogging or lifting weights. If you are in the fitness world then you know there are 3 kinds of training. **(1) Cardiovascular Exercise:** Defined as any kind of exercise that raises the heart rate for more than 20 minutes straight. It is important to get some cardiovascular exercise, but many overdue this and spend Qi they don't have. Look at the longevity of joggers and you will see that running, especially in the heat, is more draining of longevity than it is good for health. Cardiovascular exercise should be done on a race track, beach sand, or a field, like soccer to be natural and health promoting. Qigong, especially the way it is taught in this L-1 form, is effective to cardiovascular health in profound ways and does not induce a stress response. **(2) Muscular Strength**: For most people, going to the gym is how they build muscular strength. My uncle is a carpenter and builds houses all day long. He can bend a crow bar and never has touched a weight in his life. Resistance training, like weight lifting, can be very useful for health if it is not overdone. I recommend doing Qigong beforehand to lessen the effects of cortisol and stress on the body. Long ago I used to bench press 250 pounds weighing myself just 130 lbs. I gave up lifting weights 10 years ago, because I truly desired the third kind of strength most. **(3) Muscular Endurance:** *There are people who do 1000's of push-ups in a row without stopping*. Of course, this is an extreme case, but illustrates the type of strength I am referring to. It is the muscles ability to perform high numbers of repetition and endure. It is contingent on the muscles ability to produce ATP i.e. Electrical Energy. Standing in the forms gives the most precious type of strength—the ability of the muscles to endure for long periods. *This builds vitality, immunity and raises your level of electrical energy and ATP!* Does it sound hard? Don't worry... I am continually amazed by women in their 80's who do the entire form without a hitch. We know from experience that most people can do the form. Gradually... your Qi level will rise as you gain muscular endurance.

# Qigong Ready Position

The opening posture for all of our Qigong exercises begins with Ready Position.   It is perhaps one of the most important lessons in the program, because it is used as a foundation for everything else.   We use this posture in Qigong Walking and the five exercises within the Qigong Healing routine.  The essence is roundness.  Notice the arms are held in a rounded shape as are the hands.  This is important because the Qi will build up much stronger in this shape.   Also notice that the hands are not limp, but they are not rigid either.  The hand is held fairly open with **space between each finger**.  When the fingers touch it will diminish your ability to collect Qi.  Knees are slightly bent and feet are parallel at shoulder width.

Be patient with yourself. To be able to hold the arms and hands perfect all the time is the mark of a Qigong master.  Therefore, don't expect to get it 100% perfect right away.  Relaxation is also important and you should not become over-consumed with the perfection of posture if it makes you rigid.  You can always relax more.   After entering into the posture think about **Relaxing and sinking your shoulders**.

**Opening Procedure:** After entering Ready Position we begin practice with a warm up exercise.  As you inhale move your hands away from your thighs 3-5 inches.  During exhale they will return to the original position.  We take 9 breaths like this before starting the actual Qigong Healing routine.  It sends a signal to your mind and body that you are beginning your practice.

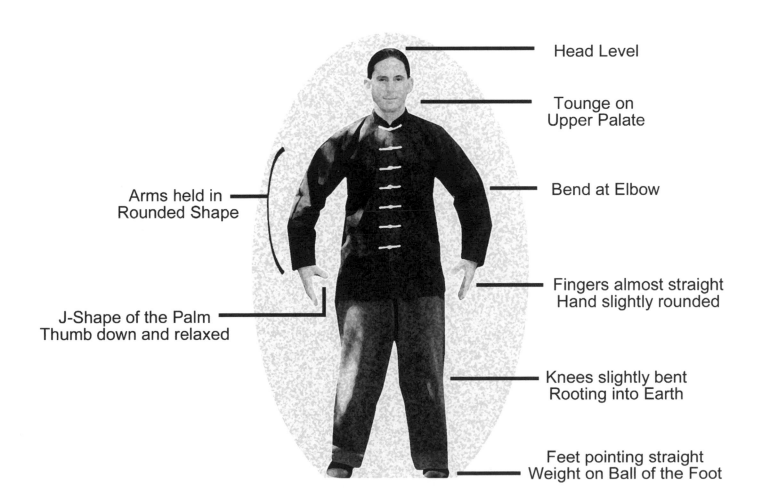

Head Level

Tounge on
Upper Palate

Bend at Elbow

Arms held in
Rounded Shape

Fingers almost straight
Hand slightly rounded

J-Shape of the Palm
Thumb down and relaxed

Knees slightly bent
Rooting into Earth

Feet pointing straight
Weight on Ball of the Foot

# Spiraling Method

Throughout the worlds great archeological sites you will find "spirals" carved into the stone. It seems that most things move in a spiral. Take a look at Mother Nature. DNA, snails, hurricanes, galaxies, and whirlpools all naturally take this shape. The life force is also moving like this in and out of your body. Using the *Spiraling Method* allows you to collect a great deal of Qi during many practices. It is rarely discussed and usually kept a secret. Most schools of Qigong teach spiraling Qi in terms of visualizing the Qi spiraling. While this has some merit, I believe the true essence of spiraling to be a subtle Qigong movement.

The movement originates from your shoulders. Begin while making small "spirals" with your hands in ready position. *(Spiraling is also used in every Qigong exercise within this workshop).* The idea is to make **perfect ovals** along the way. They get smaller progressively until you are making very small ovals at the center of the spiral. Move as if you are coaxing the Qi into your body. **The left hand turns clockwise.** While your doing this you can think about the Fog being everywhere. Think about the energy coming to your hands as you do it. The more you think about the Qi—the stronger it will get. After a short period of time you will learn to make smaller and smaller ovals. Keep a precise oval shape to the movements.

# Press on the Edge of the Energy Field ™

The Human Energy Field is tangible and able to be perceived by 98% of the people we come in contact with. It has "Elastic" qualities much like a soap bubble does. We trademarked the phrase "Press on Qi" because it was the easiest way for our students to understand this *crucial secret of Qigong*.

Universal Energy comes from the True Source. It is powerful, yet subtle. Vibratory, yet peaceful. During many of the postures within Supreme Science Qigong forms there are times when you will hear the instruction "Press on Qi" or "Press on the Edge of the Energy Field". This is describing a process of connecting with your subtle energy field and tapping into its natural connection with the universal power source.

*The pressing motion itself is almost invisible. It looks like a slight pressing motion as if to respect the integrity of a soap bubble without popping it. When we press on Qi with sincerity it immediately "pulses" Blood and Qi into the hands.*

*When we press on Qi... the elastic field of the energy bubble becomes more tangible.*

# Press on Qi ™ — While Moving!

The act of Pressing on Qi officially happens at the beginning or end of a long movement. For example, in the SSQC L-1 Qigong DVD it will say "Hold the Qi" or "Press on Qi" along with an image of the energy ball. The membrane of the energy ball will "flash brighter" at the moment pressing occurs. *I feel this is a totally unique understanding that will revolutionize Qigong and Energy for mankind.*

For the higher levels of Tai Chi and Qigong to be realized one must learn to "Press on Qi while moving." It is fairly easy for the vast majority of people to feel this "Press on Qi Mechanism" when they are standing still motionless. The stillness makes it easier to feel the edge of the energy field. However, the big *Qigong Breakthrough* occurs when the student can "Press on the Qi" throughout the entire form while moving the arms! Then in the grocery store... the bank...

# Level-1 Qigong Healing Form: "Empty Force"

It becomes clear after only two minutes of practice that this is a very powerful thing to do. It is suspected that Empty Force (a.k.a. Standing on Stake) was one of the first Qigong exercises ever conceived, and its still one of the best. It is used by thousands of Qigong and Wushu schools. It is classified as a mild form of 'Hard Qigong' because you will hold your arms in the postures for extended periods of time. This requires a minor amount of willpower, however there is a strong magnetic force that envelopes your hands and entire body, which easily gives everyone enough strength to finish the routine. Actually, the Empty Force originally given to SSQC from Paul Dong had absolutely no movement, no breath timing, no pulsing pressing or spiraling! He would just stand in the postures perfectly still like a statue for hours! I myself have found the practice to be much more powerful with the following breath, movement and relaxation techniques.

## Empty Force Posture 1A

*Arms are rounded by pointing elbows outward a little bit. Hands are at a 45 degree angle with fingertips connected energetically. Posture is held "1-hand-length" away from the belly. Feel as if you are hugging a barrel or something of similar shape.*

Inhale: Expand hands to shoulder width with fingertips pointing at each other.
Exhale: Bring hands inward towards each other—focus the energy in your palms.
We do 9 repetitions of this movement and finish with 3 horizontal spirals as shown.

*\* In between each inhale and exhale there is a "Momentary Pause" to connect with the Qi before moving again.*
*\* Try not to make the moves 'repetitiously' but rather with precise focused movements. Smooth movements have more Qi.*

## Empty Force Posture 1B

Inhale: Dip hands "down and outward" away from your body. Sloping and rising like a capital letter D. Press on Qi!™ *Fingertips point forward in this outstretched pose.*

Exhale: Holding the Qi...we press inward on it...while bending at the elbow...drawing palms toward navel. While moving hands we are directing the energy into our Lower Dan Tien in a straight line.

## Special Pulsing Exercise

After performing 9 repetitions side to side (1A) and 9 repetitions towards and away from you (1B) we will really get things cooking with the Special Pulsing Exercise. Returning to the original posture of Empty Force we softly "Pulse on the edge of the Energy Field" ™ side to side a few times. Then we pulse towards and away.
The movements are visible and gradually get smaller. We do at least 3 times in each direction. For many people this exercise begins the flow of powerful energy. Pulsing makes Qi flow stronger. See below...

Pulsing is comparable to a "particle accelerator" which is a machine physicists use to break down atoms into smaller particles. (Bet you never thought about how they did that.) They take a huge donut shaped tunnel and fill it with electrons. Powerful magnetism is turned on/off repeatedly. It is this on/off use of magnetism that "propels the atoms" to move in the tunnel. This on/off mechanism moves the atoms to such a degree that they collide into each other breaking them down into smaller particles, like quarks. When I first learned this about physics it made me smile with a huge realization. When we turn magnetism on and off in rapid succession it moves the atoms in the tunnel, but it also moves energy in our body. Pulsing is awesome!

## Empty Force Posture 2A

Transition from 1st posture to 2nd:  Inhale and slowly raise hands up to shoulder height.
Exhale RELAX and sink your shoulders.  Lower the height of the elbows below the hands.

Helpful Hints: Keep plenty of space between fingers and connect them energetically to the opposite hand.
Feel as if you are hugging your arms around a "Pillar of Qi".  It grows and contracts with your movement.

Inhale:  Expand hands to shoulder width with fingertips pointing at each other.
Exhale:  Bring hands inward towards each other—focus the energy in your palms.
    We do 9 repetitions of this movement and finish with 3 horizontal spirals.

## Empty Force Posture 2B

Inhale:  Dip hands "down and outward" away from your body. Sloping and rising like a capital letter D. Press on Qi!™ *Fingertips forward in outstretched pose.*

Exhale: Holding the Qi...we press inward on the surface of it. Bending at elbow... draw your palms toward chest center. Direct the energy into Middle Dan Tien. *Deliver Qi moving back in a straight line.*

*Feeling the energy more... Now take it a step further... Visualize the energy coming onto your chest.*

## Empty Force Posture 3A

*Think about the energy connection... from your biceps and forearms... with the skin on your face.*
*Use your mind… Mentally focus on the Qi... this increases its power... keeping arms strong and supported by the energy.*

Transition from 2nd posture to 3rd:  Inhale slowly raising hands up well above head. Palms facing forehead. Exhale RELAX and sink your shoulders.   If you cannot hold this posture slowly descend to position 1A.

Helpful Hints: After only 2 days in the workshops many people who could not do this exercise comfortably at first find that their body adapts very fast.  It is common place to get tight in the shoulders while holding the upper posture of Empty Force.  Feel that your arms are "floating" on the magnetic field around your head.

Inhale:  Expand hands to shoulder width with palms pointing at forehead.
Exhale:  Bring hands inward —focus the energy around your face.
        We do 9 repetitions of this movement and finish with 3 horizontal spirals.

## Empty Force Posture 3B

Inhale:  Dip hands "Down...Outward...High Up in the Air"! Sloping and rising like a capital letter D. Press on Qi!™ *Fingertips face the sky in outstretched pose.*

Exhale:  Bending at elbow… draw palms toward forehead. Direct the energy into Upper Dan Tien. *Deliver Qi in straight line.*

## Empty Force Posture:  The Descent

*Shape your hands as if you are "Holding a Roof-Top".*
*The 45° Degree Angle of the Palms during the descent is a powerful shape for building the Qi.*

<u>Inhale</u>:  Slowly turn hands... with fingers facing the front... palms at a 45 degree angle.

*Precise lowering of the hands leads all the "Blood and Qi" to flow powerfully throughout your body.*
*We maximize this part of Empty Force by (A) Prolonging the Exhale (B) Keeping "Top of Hands Level" as we descend.*

<u>Exhale</u>:  Press on the edge/membrane of the energy field™ while lowering the hands.
Lower the hands very slow.  Exhale for 20 seconds if you are good at breathing slow.

## Empty Force Posture:  9 Twin Spirals

<u>Free Breath Timing</u>:  After descending to base... Keeping top of hands Level... 9 large precise slow Twin Spirals.
Hands are steady and do not rise and fall.  Finger Tips face the front the entire time.
Passing through the center of the spiral hands are coming inward to bring Qi to you.

# Level-1 Qigong Healing Form: "Cloud Hands"

The energy and movements of Cloud Hands can make you feel like you're an Eagle with large wings. SSQC's version of Cloud Hands emphasizes the use of *sincere movement* and awareness of subtleties such

(1) How to hold and position the wrists.
(2) How to allow the Qi to assist the movements.
(3) How to focus and contain the Qi to facilitate maximum circulation of energy through your body.

As you practice Cloud Hands, your Lungs get used to opening bigger. The large chest expansion helps the energy of the heart and lungs. Cloud Hands naturally improves breathing and is performed 9 times.

## Cloud Hands: Inhale to Face Height

<u>Inhale</u>:  With a precise movement... Raise hands to the height of your face.

*Helpful Hints:*  *During the Initial Ascent Upward... We Adjust our Wrists... Keeping the Top of our hands "Level with the Ground".*
*After Hands reach the "Top of your Ribcage"... Lift up arms from the shoulder... Bringing Hands to Face Height.*
*Press on the surface of the Qi ™ while lifting hands.  Hold the Ball of Qi to your face... look out the Window of Life.*

## Cloud Hands:  Exhale to the Sky

<u>Exhale</u>:  Lift arms from the shoulder.  Gradually turn palms to face the front.  Hands held high into the Sky.

*Helpful Hints:*  *Feel as if you are releasing the energy up to the sky as an offering to the Universe.*
*Arrive at the top with Palm facing forward… Energy fills the "Space Between your Arms".*

## Cloud Hands:  Special Spiraling & Pulsing Exercise

<u>Free Breath Timing</u>:  During 1 or more repetitions we pause at the top for this exercise.
Spiral from the shoulders… drawing small ovals in the air above you.
Afterwards "Pulse on the edge of the energy field side-to-side". ™

*Helpful Hints:*  *Spiraling is used to draw energy into arms and hands.*
*Pulsing side-to-side amplifies the Qi Tremendously.*
*We use this exercise to facilitate advanced practice.*
*It helps "Let the Qi Move You" on the next inhale.*
*It strengthens "Press inward on Qi while moving outward".*

## Cloud Hands: Inhale Expand into an Arc of Energy

<u>Inhale</u>: Expand into an Arc with the outer base of your wrist leading. Improve the strength of the energy by "Pressing Inward on the Energy as you Expand" ™. This is a subtle technique that may take time to fully develop. Arrive in the "T-Posture" with arms extended almost 100% (but still relaxed). This is the biggest off all the Qigong postures. You are extended out like a 'T' with palms facing front.

 *Helpful Hints:* *"Gently Press on Qi Inwards as you Expand Outwards" ™*
*Using the Outer Base of your Palm... Initiate an Arc of Energy...*
*Sincere Movement is the KEY to Qigong... Expand the Energy with FEELING.*

## Cloud Hands: Exhale to Palm-Facing-Palm

<u>Brief Pause Before Exhale</u>: Bend and pivot from the elbow bringing hands forward. Point palms down.

<u>Exhale</u>: Prolong the breath and maximize this movement. Lower Arms and Arc hands inward below navel.

 *Helpful Hints:* *Bending at Elbows... Hands pass through Qi... Touch energy as hands move through it.*
*Project energy down to Earth "Palms facing Directly Down"... Lower arms from shoulder.*
*Keep a "wide" posture while lowering the hands... Bring Hands together after Navel Height.*
*Change projection of Qi... From "straight down" to "palm-facing-palm" with turning of wrists.*

# Level-1 Qigong Healing Form: "Earth Hands"

Floating Hands would be another good name for this Qigong exercise. It feels like the arms lift by themselves as Qi pours out of the palms making the practice seem effortless. Of course, the real secret is to Press on Qi ™ and Touch the Edge of the Energy Field ™ while making the movements. You may notice that SSQC instructors will make a subtle wrist adjustment when initiating the inhale or exhale. This type of move puts a 'spin' on the energy and is a form of Pressing on Qi.

This Qigong exercise is for the lower portion of the body. Collecting Qi we strengthen our hips, legs and reproductive organs. In Chinese medicine the Earth represents our legs and abdomen. When we descend our arms, Pressing on the Qi inside, ™ we create a "Grid of Qi" and release this energy to wash over our vital center. 9 repetitions in

## Earth Hands: Inhale Arcing Hands Up to Shoulder Height

Inhale: From Ready position, bring hands "Out to Side and in Front". Both directions create an arc shape allowing the hands to float up effortlessly. We finish the movement at shoulder height, fingers facing the front and with a bend in the elbow (see top image). The shape is very important.

 Helpful Hints: *When raising hands we think about energy pouring out the palms to facilitate the movement as being weightless and effortless. A subtle wrist motion may initiate the movement from ready position to put a 'spin' on the energy. At the top of the movement we arrive with a bend in the elbows and our wrists adjusted to have hands and fingers pointing straight ahead like our feet do in ready position.*

## Earth Hands: Spiral 3 Times - While Holding Breath

We incorporate a short breath hold at the top after the 4th repetition. "Spiraling is always followed by Pressing" ™ is a teaching that is fundamental to the SSQC system of Qigong. Three spirals draw energy around the arms. Pressing creates a "Sheet of Qi" that we then lower and carry to our vital organs.

Helpful Hints: *Allow the spirals to originate from your shoulders. Think about your arms/fingers moving through the "Universal Energy Plasma" surrounding us.*

## Earth Hands Reps 1-3: Exhale Brushing Fingertips over the Surface of Qi

<u>Exhale</u>:  While lowering the hands think about the Qi Plasma all around us and hands moving through it. Brush down fingertips over the surface of the energy. Come down and return to ready position.

 ***Helpful Hints:*** *Initiate the movement by "adjusting wrist slightly" to raise fingertips higher than base of palm.  This subtle wrist adjustment helps us to strengthen the energy connection and enhance Brushing Down.*

## Earth Hands Reps 4-9: Exhale Carrying the "Grid of Energy"

  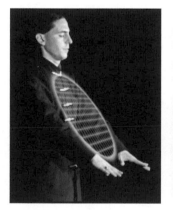 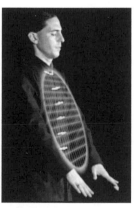

<u>Exhale</u>:  While lowering the hands "Press Inward on the Qi" ™  Use a soft pressure on the membrane of the energy field to contain the Qi in between your biceps and forearms.  As you softly lower hands passing through the Qi... feel you are carrying the Qi down to drape over lower body.

# Level-1 Qigong Healing Form: "Around the World"

Ancient Qigong practitioners have used variations of this exercise to build energy for 1000's of years. You will create a sphere of Qi by repeatedly rotating palms over the surface of a ball. Shortly, it will begin to have mass and take on a structure like a dense ball of electrons vibrating in your hands. We make rotations 180° Degrees with both our hands as they turn over the surface of the ball... and in the waist changing the direction we face.

It has been observed that many high level Qigong Healers use ball making rotations similar to this exercise for giving their patients healing. Also noteworthy is the waist rotations help improve the digestion/elimination systems. Some have called this system "Colon Cleansing Qigong". Of course, when we rotate slowly 180 degrees from our waist it stirs up the junk inside us. Especially when slow breathing is used in timing with your movements.

From ready position, <u>Inhale</u>: Turn palms facing forward and lift until parallel to the ground.
<u>Exhale</u>: While rotating the palms to face each other.
<u>Inhale & Exhale</u>: 3 times while doing the "Open and Close" movement.

<u>Inhale</u>: "Ball-Holding Posture" is formed by Rotating Arms and Hands. Right hand is on Top.
"1-Hand-Length" away from the body is the distance we keep Palm-over-Palm connection.
"Round Out the Lower Arm" so elbow is gently pointed outward.
"Relax Upper Shoulder" by sinking the Elbow lower than hand.

<u>Exhale</u>: Turn from your waist and "Carry the Qi" to your left side.

**ALL IS ONE 36**

# Level-1 Qigong Healing Form: "Around the World"

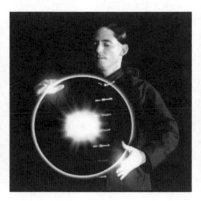

*"Press on the Surface of the Energy Ball"™ while rotating hands over the edge of it.*

From Left Side, <u>Inhale</u>: Rotate your hands "around the edge" of a perfectly shaped sphere.
<u>Pause</u>:  With precise movement..."Press on the Qi Diagonally" ™

<u>Exhale</u>:  Turn from waist and carry the Qi to center for the "Diagonal Pulsing Exercise".

From Center, <u>Inhale</u>:  Expand both arms outward in a Diagonal Direction.
<u>Exhale</u>:  Slowly bring them back into the Ball-Holding Posture.
<u>Free Breath Timing</u>:  "Pulse back and forth gently on the edge of the energy field" ™
"Diagonally pulse on/off the membrane of the energy field" ™

*The Diagonal Pulsing Exercise really makes the Energy Strong!*

# Level-1 Qigong Healing Form: "Around the World"

<u>Exhale From Center to Right Side</u>:  Rotate from your waist and "glide over" to the other side.
*Use the principle of "Press Diagonally while Moving" to carry the sphere over to the other side.

<u>Inhale</u>:  Change Hands... Gloss palms over the surface of a perfect sphere.
Notice that Palms are always 180° degrees across from each other.
This keeps the energetic "Palm-facing-Palm" connection maximized.
At the top of the Inhale... after changing hands... Press on Qi Diagonally™

<u>Exhale from Left to Right Side</u>: Rotate from waist 180 degrees. *Press on Qi while moving!*

# Level-1 Qigong Healing Form: "Around the World"

  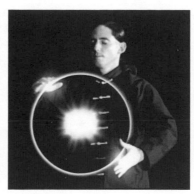 

\*\*\* We visit each side 6 times for a total of 12 repetitions.
\*\*\* Try to perform the rotations at the waist *without moving your head up and down*.
\*\*\* Diagonal Pulsing Exercise ™ is performed in the center position at least twice.
\*\*\* After you finish the last repetition come back to center to end the exercise.

From Center, <u>Inhale</u>: Change Hands and lower "forearms level with floor". Point Palms Down...
<u>Exhale</u>: Slowly lower hands down projecting energy outward and into the Earth.

# Level-1 Qigong Healing Form: "Push Hands"

The Supreme Science Qigong system utilizes a unique concept in the Push Hands exercise. We call it *"Sending Energy from 1 Hand to the Other"* ™ and it involves the "mental direction" of energy to another hand. The result is that the receiving hand has "Double Qi" and now pulses twice as strong as before (because it has the energy of 2 hands). As crazy as that might sound, the feeling is so profound from *"Sending Energy from 1 Hand to the Other"* ™ that it can literally assist in your body's movement during a 180 degree rotation to the other side. With more practice "Your force of Qi" will gradually increase. The ancient Qigong expression says, "Let the Qi move you."

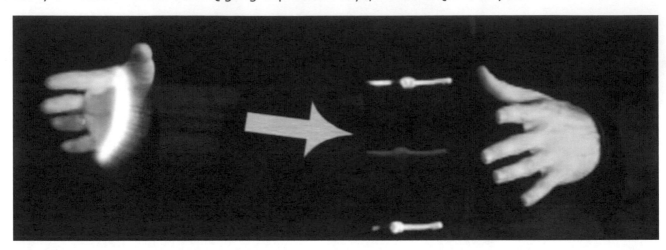

*The Secret to Qigong Push Hands is to "Press on Qi While Moving" ™ with the Transmitting Hand (left in photo)*
*The Receiving Hand (right in photo) will "Pulsate with Double Qi" as Qi from the Transmitting Hand lands on it.*

From ready position, <u>Inhale</u>: Turn palms facing forward and lift until parallel to the ground.
<u>Exhale</u>: While rotating the palms to face each other.
<u>Inhale & Exhale</u>: 3 times while doing the "Open and Close" movement.

<u>Inhale</u>: Pull back 'right' hand. Keep left hand stationary to "Receive Qi from Transmitting Hand".
<u>Exhale</u>: Spiral (slow-precise circles) from Elbow 3 Times. *Think about Qi traveling to the Receiving Hand.*
While still exhaling, turn to the left side allowing the "Force of Qi" to assist your movement.

**ALL IS ONE** *40*

# Level-1 Qigong Healing Form: "Push Hands"

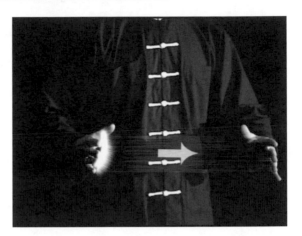

*Turning from waist 180° Degrees to the other side is a long journey. If you can exhale the entire time you're very good at Qigong. If you are new to Qigong you can breathe twice during this waist rotation. Don't rush the movement. Its better to breathe twice. During this rotation to the other side… Use your Mind… "Think about energy going from 1 hand to the other".* ™

Inhale: Pull back 'left' hand. Keep right hand stationary to "Receive Qi from Transmitting Hand".
Exhale: Spiral (slow-precise circles) from Elbow 3 Times. *Think about Qi traveling to the Receiving Hand.*
      While still exhaling, *turn to the right* side allowing the "Force of Qi" to assist your movement.

*When pulling the Transmitting Hand back on the Inhale… adjust the wrist to create a precise palm-facing-palm connection. Keep forearms "Level with the Floor" during the entire practice. Elbows are bent at 90° Degrees. This helps you relax more.*

Inhale: Pull back 'right' hand. Keep left hand stationary to "Receive Qi from Transmitting Hand".
Exhale: Spiral (slow-precise circles) from Elbow 3 Times. *Think about Qi traveling to the Receiving Hand.*
      While still exhaling, turn to the left side allowing the "Force of Qi" to assist your movement.

    *** We visit each side 6 times for a total of 12 repetitions.
    *** Perform the rotations at the waist *without moving your head up and down*.
    *** Upon returning to center we enter "Closing Procedure" skipping the Ready Position.

# Level-1 Qigong Healing Form: "Closing Procedure"

Ancient Chinese statures like this one can be found throughout China. They also grace the entrance to many American Chinese Restaurants. The warrior is holding his hands over the Dan Tien in the closing Qigong posture. Some schools of Qigong will have closing procedures that are over 20 minutes long!! The more advanced your Qigong becomes the greater the emphasis on closing. The Level-2 form uses the "9-Breath Method", which is an advanced Pranayama closing practice. Both Level-1 and Level-2 closing procedures involve breathing mechanics, and turning your focus inward to your Qi. These practices are extremely important because they "tell your body that your practice is complete and to seal away the energy inside your lower Dan Tien". You're **concentrating** the Qi and putting it away in the lower Dan Tien for storage. This is the best place to keep surplus energy.

**Inhale,** expand hands outward w/fingertips leading. **Exhale,** bring hands inward with base of palm leading.
*There is a subtle wrist adjustment that occurs here. Repeat the open and close movement 3 times.

**Inhale,** bring your right hand on top in the ball-holding posture.
**Free Breath Timing**, rotate your palms "Pressing on the Surface of the Energy Ball" ™
We make approximately 15 rotations... getting smaller, closer to body and lower down.
"Its like turning the lid off a jar" as you rotate mostly from your wrist after a short time.

## Closing Posture and 9 Qigong Breaths

After the wrist rotations have compacted the energy into a small sphere.... Ladies bring left hand on top... Gentleman right. Think about putting all your good ideas and intentions going into the ball. Cover the navel center with palm-over-palm posture. Take 1-5 minutes for 9 Peaceful Qigong Breaths. These are filling lowest part of your abdomen first. Think slow breathing.

**ALL IS ONE** *42*

# Taoist Stretching

These are unique "warrior style" stretches to keep your body flexible and strong. We practice our Taoist stretching routine during long Qigong routines to help the energy flow better. Some of the exercises come from yoga, some are isometric push/pull stretches and others are from high school wrestling. The routine covers every major muscle in the body and can be gradually worked towards as some stretches may not be fully accessible to all people. Only do what you can. Love it all.

### #1 Bent Knee Hamstring Stretch

With back leg bent at the knee and other leg stretched out fully... Grab your big and second toe firmly. You're really grabbing them. Press thumb into the acupoint in between the first 2 toes. Place other hand gently on top of the knee keep it down to the ground. While pulling on the toes and pressing the acupoint lean forward for 3-5 seconds. Take a breather for a few seconds and lean back, but don't let go of the toes. Lean forward and do one more stretch. Change sides for a total of 2 times each side.

### #2A  L-Shaped Hamstring Stretch

This stretch has its inverse with the Quad Stretch below. That means they alternate from A to B and then repeat. These inverse stretches are AWESOME because they stretch and develop your muscle fibers in complimentary directions. i.e. the quads and hamstrings should be stretched within the same 20 seconds.

Grabbing the first 2 toes firmly like before... stretch your leg high up to the best of your ability. Feel free to go past the L-shape and bring the foot farther back if you can.   Two times each side.

### #2B Push-Pull Quad Stretch

After doing stretch 2A... grab the top of your entire foot and put it behind you.  Pull "backwards using your arm strength". Feel the stretch in your quads. Push "forward with your leg strength". You are creating a push/pull stretch using your arm strength and your leg strength.  This really opens the muscle fibers of your legs. Alternate and do 2A and 2B then 2A and 2B.  Then change sides and two to more sets on the other leg.

## #3A Feet Together Inner Thigh Stretch

Bring your feet together with the soles touching, Clasp the toes and interlock fingers over the tops of the feet. Slowly inch the feet inwards towards your body. It is a gentle inner thigh stretch.

## #3B Rounding & Lengthening Spine Stretch

Without letting go of the feet... Release the stretch by curving your spine and leaning back as far as you can. This straightens your arms and stretches your entire upper shoulders. Then pull yourself forward sticking your chest out even higher than before. This is stretching your inner thigh again and also your lower back. Alternate 2 times.

## #4A Foot Goes Up and Back Stretch

Extend legs out and bring one foot near you to grab. Hold firmly w/2 hands. Slowly pull the foot closer to your body. Gradually lift it up another inch and then bring it back. Its up and back in small increments. Feel it open the gluts, which probably could use some stretching after standing in Qigong postures. One day you might be able to touch your nose. Alternate this stretch with 4B to really make the legs powerful. Be forewarned that the stretch below is the most difficult of all. Go slow if needed. 2 times each.

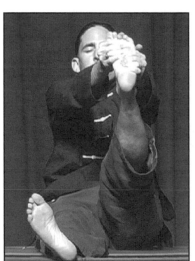

## #4B Straighten Leg Holding Foot Stretch

This is the one stretch that beginners will want to go slow on. Simply straighten your leg slowly while holding the foot. It's a real burn. Afterwards your legs feel like totally new legs! Alternate twice each side.

**ALL IS ONE** *44*

## #5A Child's Pose Back Stretch

Everyone knows this pose from yoga. Its one of my favorites because it releases so much stress from the lower back. Bring knees up into chest and touch your eyebrow center to the mat. Gradually inch your fingers farther away. Visualize steam rising off your back. After 15 seconds lean forward to the alternating pose, the cobra. Alternate 2 times.

## #5B Cobra Abdominal Stretch

There are 2 versions of this exercise. One version is like you see pictured left. Tops of feet rest on the mat. Thighs touch the mat. Second version is harder with legs off the mat and supported by your toes. In both versions the arms straighten to raise upper body off the mat. This stretches your abdominal muscles in contrast to your lower back from child's pose. Think about your abdomen opening and stretching more. Look up and raise chin.

## #6 Kidney Lose Hand Pounding

Pound with light-medium force on the lower back with lose fists. Go all the way up and down as far as you can. 2 minutes is great. Your whole body may vibrate afterwards. That is a good sign that you moved a lot of energy in this area. Kidneys time to wake up.

## #7 Sword Finger Bicep/Chest Stretch

With index and middle fingers touching (like swords) bring arms out to side. Keep the sword fingers "pointed up" to the sky. Now stretch to the side more. Like you are trying to reach the edges of the room. Then bring back your hands fully stretched behind you a few more inches. Release the stretch gracefully and slowly. We do this one time.

## #8 Grab Elbow Shoulder Stretch

Grab above your elbow and pull the arm slowly to stretch deltoids. When you pull left… you look right. You can gradually pull the arm harder to get a deeper stretch. Stretch each shoulder separately two times.

## #9 Hand over Kidneys Chest Stretch

Bring hands over kidneys and then draw elbows in. Stick out your chest and feel all the muscles across your chest and shoulders open and release. One time.

## #10 Hulk Rounding Back Stretch

Hold arms out wide in front of you. Then make a large "rounding" gesture with your back. Feel that your entire back is opening and that any stress rises up off you like steam. Hold this stretch for 10 to 20 seconds. One time.

## #11 Fist Forward Side Back Stretch

Directly from the Hulk Rounding stretch… pull one hand back in a fist and reach forward with other hand. Reach…Reach… Reach…

After five seconds lean to the side opposite your extended hand. This stretches the large side muscles of the back. Each side two times.

## #12 Shoulder Rotations

Lift up both shoulders together and roll them back. Go slowly making a full rotation as far as your body permits. This one helps to loosen the entire back Do nine rotations each direction. This concludes the Taoist Stretching routine.

# Qigong Walking

Perhaps the most important discovery since the computer, Qigong Walking allows you to practice anytime, anywhere, and if your good you can conceal it and no one will be able to tell. If you do not enjoy walking then perhaps you should re-think that. Most of the great masters from the scriptures around the world have journeyed away from the village for great lengths of time on foot. Walking puts a stride in place that circulates the energy from the sacrum and spirals it up and down the spine. Walking is the ultimate way of Qi circulation since it gets blood moving physically yet allows the mind to remain calm and focus inward. Walking cannot be substituted for running - or any other activity. You can practice whether your walking on the beach, shopping in the grocery store, or following a jogging session as the "cool down" walk (this is especially powerful). As for practical application it does not get any more useful than this. Now you can practice anytime/anywhere without a planned practice setting. Just simply go for a walk!

## Breathing and Walking Simultaneously

The challenge is to breathe in the given method and walk naturally at the same time. This takes practice, but you'll get it to be natural in a short time period. Remember to breath deeply into your lower abdomen and pull the abdomen back towards the spine as you exhale (3-pt breathing). You'll notice the effects when your hands begin to pulsate stronger than usual. The blood will begin to flow very powerfully to your hands and you may begin to sweat and tingle. This is good because it means the Qi is moving strong. Do not perform Qigong Walking in direct sun when it gets hot outside. I sometimes go between 7-8AM to avoid getting over heated.

## Magnetics & Hand Posture

The Level-1 Qigong walking practice uses the ready stance posture. The hands need to be kept "loosely opened" in order to keep the Lao Gong point open. This is probably the most important aspect of the Qigong walk. "Limp Hands" cannot gather Qi efficiently. You'll notice right away the difference when your hands are opened and round with thumbs relaxed. Hand posture makes a huge difference in all Qigong practices, especially the walk. Check out the picture for details on the correct posture. Your hands and arms are rounded as if you were actually carrying something. A big ball of Qi will form and get heavy. People often describe it as so thick and tangible that is has taken "physical mass". The hands will sometimes feel like oil is coming out of the palms because so much blood is circulating into the hands. After you get warmed up and your Qi is really cooking of you should be able to slow down your breathing. This will make your movements very subtle. In Level-3 we teach how to disguise the Walking Qigong practice so that no one will know your doing it. You will simply appear focused. Once you can disguise it you have reached a higher level in your ability to collect Qi.

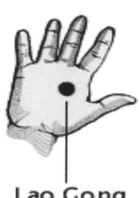

Lao Gong

# Bone Marrow Washing — While Walking

This practice has stood the test of time with our students. We all agree this is one of the favorites. It is preformed during Qigong Walking and again in Wuji Style Qigong. It is a 'Washing' type of movement. It helps keep the energy of your body flowing powerfully while walking. Our preference is to practice this exercise frequently because of its power.

1) Standard Qigong Walking Posture
2) Inhale - Turn right palm to front.
3) Continue Inhaling - Raise <u>right</u> hand to parallel with ground.
4) Exhale - flip right hand so palm is facing left ***"inner elbow point"***.
5) Continue Exhaling - stroking right hand down left forearm beyond fingers.
6) Return to standard walking posture.
7) Inhale - Turn left palm to front.
8) Continue Inhaling - Raise <u>left</u> hand to parallel with ground.
9) Exhale, flip left hand so palm faces right ***"inner elbow point"***.
10) Continue exhaling - stroking left hand down right forearm beyond fingers. ***
    Return to standard walking posture and Repeat.

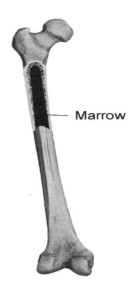

Marrow

It is said that the "essence" of our being is found within the bone marrow. Many Qigong practices focus energy to stimulate the bone marrow. Science knows that White blood cells and our entire immune system are regulated by the bone marrow. In bone breathing meditation we draw energy into the marrow and breathe from there. In washing style movements, which are used throughout the SSQ system, we focus on scanning and cleaning the actual marrow in our bones. We know the mind leads the Qi. And so this is a very powerful way to stimulate our immune system.

# Concealing your Qigong Walk

For thousands of years Qigong has been kept highly secretive. Ancient masters developed Qigong methods that could be practiced out in the open, yet be concealed. Qigong Walking is difficult to conceal and takes a lot of practice, but it can be done. The method for total concealment is called "Free-Hands" Method. It requires that a person has become very familiar with all other Qigong Walking practices beforehand. Everything else must be mastered first. After you can feel strong Qi and conceal your practice - you have reached a very high level in your Qigong. I consider this one of the main aspects of the term 'Qigong Master' since this delineates someone who is always practicing.

# Instructions

**Step 1:** After you have a lot of Qi, begin doing the basic walking method while keeping <u>one</u> shoulder still. The other shoulder is allowed to swing naturally back and forth.

**Step 2:** Use your mind. Think about the fact that your stationary hand is sending out Qi. Think about your swinging hand passing through this emitted Qi like a scanner. Feel the Qi from the stationary hand as your swinging hand "passes through it." **The swinging hand is moving in an long oval shape.** Think about this and do for 5 minutes before moving on to step 3.

**Step 3:** After you have been feeling the Qi in your swaying hand—free the stationary arm. As the left hand swings forward—your right hand swings backward. **You will consciously swing the arms in an elongated oval (cigar) shape. Open space between fingers and think about both hands collecting Qi.** You will feel the Qi getting stronger as you pass palm over palm. It feels like sparks created as palms pass by each other. The left hand is circling clockwise while the right hand is circling counterclockwise. After you have successfully been able to swing both hands freely and still maintain a cohesive energy field—then you can relax the shoulders and hands even more. Now you're only using your mind. Walking normally, you can feel the Qi building very strong by thinking about it emitting from the hands. Sway the arms naturally, not like a robot. Each pass of the hand moves all the way in front and behind you. This means you are taking more space and gives it a little bit of attitude to your walk. I walked Manhattan in a single concealing my practice everywhere I went.

*Note: This practice is probably the most difficult of all Walking methods.*
*In order to be successful you need to have already understood previous walking techniques.*
*Remember the Qi is like fog and is all around you. Think about this.*

# Qigong Meditation (Internal Qigong)

There are many methods that you can use to absorb Qi from the universal energy field (Sea of Qi). "Internal Methods" are methods of absorption that do not require physical movement. They use a principle referred to as the 'Qigong Heart/Mind'. These kind of Qigong practices will build the strength of your Shen. You can use the *will power* of the mind to direct surrounding energies into your body. The feelings and images created during Qigong meditation instruct your energy to do certain things. Many of the images presented in our meditation have been used for nearly 5000 years within Taoist Internal Alchemy.

The transformations that take place during internal practice are on the subtle Qi dimensions. This means that everything we visualize is actually happening on the astral plane (4th Dimension). The explanation for the often miraculous results of Qigong is that the astral body (energy body) is totally influenced by the mind. That is why we can think about a lemon and our body produces saliva. We can think about our feet and the Qi goes there. We can think about our Liver and the Qi goes there. Our mind has the power to heal.

# Full-Body Breathing

This meditation uses an esoteric breathing technique referred to as "Full-Body" Breathing. This involves breathing from the pores of your skin over your entire body. The entire surface area of your skin becomes an apparatus for absorbing Qi. This ancient practice is among the greatest of Taoist Qigong secrets and is very powerful. Full-Body Breathing is working with a different kind of Qi than the other practices you've learned so far and has even been shown to induce the "Bigu" state. It draws on a highly refined energy. Thus, both internal and external Qigong should be practiced to receive both kinds of Qi.

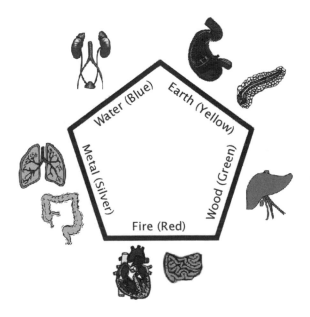

# Guidelines

1) Sit on the front 1/3rd of the chair (Genitals are hanging over the edge)

2) Spine is straight and chin is down slightly.

3) Sink your shoulders. Relax your shoulders.

4) Keep your tongue on the upper palate.

5) Resist the temptation to scratch or fidget.

6) Focus on slow 3-part breathing.

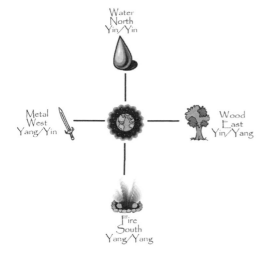

# Taoist Five Elemental Theory

Within the heart of the Tao lies the theory of the Five Elements. Their use is very diverse and spans from healing to understanding human relationships. It is a cross cultural tool that works well for adjusting ones lifestyle to better suit the individual needs of the body. The basic premise of 'Taoist Five Elemental Theory' is that we all are more heavily attributed towards certain elements and lacking in others. We are all more one single element than the rest. This is powerful information to know about yourself and your body. It can help you understand what your needs really are. The Five Elements of the Tao are: Wood, Fire, Metal, Water, and Earth. We will briefly discuss each element since their significance in Qigong is profound.

# Five Elemental Theory for the Body & Human Behavior

**Wood:** The technical name for this element is 'wood', however it is better said as 'Tree' since the living representation provides a much better description. The Tree is the "giver" and the first element in the life cycle. Most children are 'Tree-like' in their innocent behavior. The tree is the one who wants to love and give. The wood feeds the Fire. If the liver (wood organ) has problems then there is not enough wood for the fire (energy). Cleansing the liver brings new energy (fire). Furthermore, if the water element is missing (kidney) and there is too much Fire (High Blood Pressure), the tree cannot be nourished fast enough by the water. They are all connected. Tree or Wood is the most missing element in today's society. Metal is the strongest in our times of government and corporate way of life. The metal excess 'cuts down' (opposes) the Tree. Metal blade is notorious for cutting trees. People who have too much Tree Energy are characterized by giving so much that they become depleted. Anger is the emotion that depletes the Tree/Wood Energy.

**Fire:** When the body is too Yang (Fire), the skin of the face is often dry and red. The skin becomes dry because the Fire (Heart) is drying out the water (Kidney). This is a common among Americans who eat a diet high in animal protein. Meat is the Fire in the food kingdom. When a person eats too much meat for his/her constitution, the body builds up too much internal heat and dries out. The 'unlimited energy' people are Fire types. The Fire might be prone to use the stimulating effects of Coffee or Rigorous Exercise to stimulate the 'Adrenal Glands'. This is stimulating the Kidneys (which are the storage tanks for the body's Qi) to release Qi in the blood stream. Adrenaline junkies love to skydive because of the adrenal high they get to borrow, but not without a price. The Fire people live the shortest lifespan since they are burning the candle at both ends. The personality of the Fire is to get things done. Make it happen. Wealthy people are almost always Fire/Metal types. The Fire and Metal go together hand in hand. The police officer is a perfect example of that. He/she has the Strength and Power of the Fire and the structure (metal) of the law backing it up. There is nothing wrong with the Metal/Fire type as these are the worker bees of the world. The risk of being a fire person is getting burnt out early in life. The hallmark of Fire types is they enjoy staying up late.

**Metal:** Characterized by the notion of structure and order. Metal is the opposite of the Tree, which frolics freely in communion with spirit. The 'Mind' is the metal of ourselves. Licensing, Regulations, Government, are pure demonstrations of the metal energy. People who are metal excessive are usually quite anal in their behavior. They are the neat freaks, the team leaders, and may have a written schedule on vacation. The metal element has many positive features. It is the essence of will power and focus required for success in Qigong. Metal brings order.

The free spirited hippies (coincidentally called 'tree huggers') sometimes have a strong negative judgment to the metal energy since it opposes the freeness of the tree, however the other side of that coin is the tree people need to learn to focus and organize better. Those who are 'anal retentive' or have any obsessive compulsive disorder are displaying the excessive metal. The best thing for excess metal is to learn from children and embrace spontaneity. Bear in mind that metal is such a strong force in human beings today, there are not many of us left who are deficient in metal. *What needs to happen is alchemization into a higher quality of metal energy. The old alchemists that were trying to transform lead into gold— were really talking about transforming the desires or focus of ones life.*

*We all have things we are disciplined with – things that matter to us. The ancient "turn lead into gold" parable is meant to define the inner transformation that occurs with cultivation. Cultivation is true sharing and living for the sake of helping others. This "Gold Metal Energy" is used to focus will power on desires that are more inclusive of society rather than just the individual or ones genetic family. Seeing globally rather than individually. This process of cultivation is a redirection of priorities and what we consider important in life. Everyone who pays their taxes and holds a job has metal energy (hence it is not deficient in modern times). Alchemy is a refining process as to "how we apply our willpower". It directly relates to removing all obstacles that oppose a spiritually fulfilling life. This is a mental choice. Metal. It is planting the flag in the ground and saying what you will do and then utilizing a mind-state of "firm willpower" to manifest it on the material plane.*

**Water:** The water is characterized by 'formlessness'. Water takes on any shape and is the 'cooling' energy. Represents the notion of wisdom and patience. Calm and relaxed people are water types. Water is usually introverted and enjoys reading very much. Reading is a water activity and so is meditation. Water people are often lacking the Fire to get out and do more rigorous (Yang) activity. Water is the most Yin element and the last of the life cycle represented by elderly (wisdom) times. The water is the philosopher and the scholar, without which life would be just about 'having fun' without greater meaning.

Excessive water leads to dampness in the body. Dampness leads to cold hands and feet, Candida bacteria, and getting sick frequently. The water excess suppresses the fire of life. We cannot sit all day long in a chair! The water must be moving. And while water is patient, water deficient people are more concerned about the immediate gratification rather than long term happiness and peace, which can only be found in spirit (water). Being too much water (meditation, reading, fruits and vegetables) will 'Yin Out' if it is not kept in balance with other Fire activities like exercise and Qigong. There are Qigong exercises for 'steaming' the water by generating Fire. The water excess needs to adopt a more active and extroverted lifestyle and not get carried away with eating too many fruits.

**Earth:** The Earth is characterized by the "Saint/Qigong Master". The Earth element is the perfect harmonization of the previous four elements in 25% shares. The idea behind Five Elemental theory is that you are supposed to 'cultivate' your personality until you are balanced in all four archetypes. The Earth person can run a marathon, sit in silence for great lengths without discomfort, gives and receives freely, and can accomplish anything or nothing if they choose. It represents true balance.

# Sea of Qi

## By: Jeff Primack

The Life Force is all around us.
A veritable "Sea of Qi" that never diminishes.
It has always been...and will always be.
From the beginning of time... up until now...
The secret has been right under your nose.
The cosmic healing breath!
Legendary throughout the ages.
From one sage passed on to another.
Generation after generation.
The ancient wisdom has endured time.

Ancients have said the Qi is like Fog.
Chinese paintings...they always have Fog.
Moving like a haze over the mountain.
Electro-Magnetic vibrations.
Tangible to those who know the way.
A most beautiful and strange way this energy behaves.
Its nature is Elusive.
Like reaching out to grab a handful of Fog...
If you don't do it carefully,
You'll push the Qi out of your hand.
Gracefulness, the first law of Qigong.

Your hand is a solar panel.
Passing through the air, you feel it.
Bring your consciousness to the Sea.
You connect.
It feels like strands of magnetism.
A subtle spiral opens the gate further.
The presence is getting stronger.
You are reminded of your true nature.
Of the non-physical self, which you play with.
Bringing a deeper awareness of life.

# Level-2 Workshop

*Advanced Breathing & Movement Applications*

# Introduction: Level-2 Qigong Healing Form

Many people will ask the question: "Which form is better to practice L-1 or L-2?" For some there are not enough hours in the day to practice both forms.  The best approach in the beginning is to spend more time on Level-1 and do the Level-2 form when there is extra time.  Or you can always do whatever you want and follow your heart. *I do recommend following the L-1 form for 90 days everyday in the short term so that you can master it.*  Level-2 is more mentally demanding, physically demanding, and uses all the foundations from Level-1 with more regularity and assumes you have understood certain principles. These principles would include: Leading Qi with your mind, push hands style techniques and more understanding of how breathing mechanics effect Qi flow.

1) **Full Body Cleansing**
2) **Drawing the Bow**
3) **Full Body Spiraling**
4) **Nine Breath Method**

# Level-2 Qigong Healing Form: "Full-Body Cleansing"

The first exercise of Level-2 is used to improve the flow of Qi and remove blockages along the body. First, the exercise opens with a gesture of receiving Qi with palms facing up. The arms rise upward from the shoulder and the palms "pass through the Qi". At the top we spiral, expand and look to the skyline with gratitude. This is a key moment in the practice. Pressing on Qi we ask and receive the great gift from the True Source. During the descent along the front of the body we employ visualization of light or a waterfall cleansing us. Heat and pulsation follows your mind down out the soles of feet. Yeah... its that good.

<u>Preparation</u>: From Ready position, bring hands "Out to Side Palms Facing Up". Keep a nice bend in the elbow. We take a moment to feel the energy connection between our arms. Pulse gently to increase Qi. This is the receiving posture to ask the Divine Source for the blessing in your practice (optional).

<u>Inhale</u>: Lift arms from your shoulders without moving from the elbow. Hands and Arms move straight up until they get to "Chest Height" in picture 3. Once at chest height we arc our arms up overhead into the third posture of empty force. Bring awareness to your arms moving through the energy.

 *Helpful Hints:* *When raising hands we think about our hands moving through a "Mist" of Qi around us. Feel that the air around you is filled with energy. Moving slower is better. The roundness of the arm is also very important. Qi likes the round shape. When moving past chest height we "scoop the energy" up into the empty force posture. It's a round arcing movement.*

You can choose to make this movement sacred. Lean back with sincerity and reverence for the "True Source".

You can choose to be in the mind-state of receiving and allowing the blessing to enter.

<u>Exhale</u>: Relax shoulders and spiral upwards gathering Qi 3 times.

<u>Inhale</u>: Expand space between palms and gently look up 45 degrees.

 *Helpful Hints:* *When you expand your hands... make a slight wrist adjustment to stimulate Qi. When you lean back... its minimal. Don't compress your neck too far back. Notice that arms are "Rounded" i.e. not in a v-shape.*

**ALL IS ONE  56**

# Level-2 Qigong Healing Form: "Full-Body Cleansing"

<u>Exhale</u>: Bend at elbows... Bend knees and root down solid.
Head level once again and look out to the horizon.

<u>Inhale</u>: Raise hands a few inches.
Press on Qi and focus mind.

<u>Long Exhale</u>: Begin by focusing attention at the crown of your head. As you slowly lower hands visualize the Qi is washing your face, chest and on downwards over your entire body. See the area where the light hits your body "crackling and burning" any stress you might have inside you. It is also important to "Press on Qi while lowering". *Follow it down with your mind.* See it blast out the soles of the feet. When your mind reaches your feet... they will get hot and pulse with blood and Qi! That is how you know this exercise is working its magic.

 ☯ **Helpful Hints:** *Notice the first 3 images on the second row. Palms are held at a 45 degree angle to the body. This angle helps to capture more Qi on the descent. Also observe that from chest to navel center the index fingers are facing each other. This isolates the wrist and strengthens the Qi considerably. Fingers point horizontal till navel.*

*The Rooting Point takes most of our weight in the Level-1 and 2 forms. This exercise has a special deviation where you "shift your weight" to the back of your foot known as the Heel Point. Weight shifts from the front to the back of the foot as hands move down past the navel (see pictures 3 and 4). You can see in pictures 4,5,6 that I progressively lean back farther. This is achieved not by deliberately leaning, but by changing the part of my foot that holds the weight. Your temporarily modified weight distribution allows your feet to pulse and release energy much more effectively.*

*Synchronizing the flow of hand rotation, shifting weight and visualization is the key. After passing navel in picture 3, index finger connection comes undone and wrists rotate allowing fingers to point down. Ideally, your weight is shifted backwards at the same speed it takes to rotate your wrists fully. You will be in the lower posture of Earth hands at picture 6. The blast of energy out your feet, the rotation of the wrists and the shift back... all happen as one synchronized flow.*

# Level-2 Qigong Healing Form: "Full-Body Cleansing"

<u>Inhale</u>: Raise arms as 1 unit by lifting from shoulders. Allow the "pull of Qi" to shift your weight forward again onto the bubbling spring point. It's a synchronized move. As the arms are risen your weight slowly returns forward on to the ball of your foot. In picture 1 you can see my body leaning back and then return rooted as I lift arms.

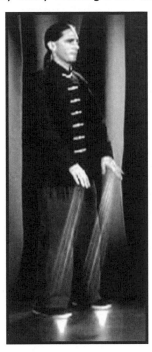 

<u>Exhale</u>: Spiral energy down to your feet (left hand clockwise). Visualize that energy is going from your hands to your feet and then the feet are emitting Qi into ground. Spiral slowly sending Qi 3 times. Return to ready position and repeat exercise. Six times total.

**☯ Helpful Hints:** *For extra credit you can spiral more than three times. Close your eyes and think about connecting with the "Center of the Earth". Other rocky planets like Mars are dead planets. But our Earth is alive from the inside. Think about sending energy to the Dan Tien of the Earth while spiraling. This is a powerful connection.*

# Level-2 Qigong Form: "Drawing the Bow"

Drawing the Bow is the most complex of the movement-based Qigong methods taught in our system. It combines everything from push hands, rotations of the wrist similar to the closing procedure, projection style movements, hard style Qigong conditioning with a lower stance, shifting the body weight like Tai Chi, visualizing Qi going from one hand to the other—this exercise will maximizing your Qi Energy!! Consider that you can do less repetitions and also raise the stance if going too far down is making the exercise impossible. I suggest doing what you can and having fun. This is the most potent of all the Qigong dealing with strength and developing external energy. The legs become strong like a horse in a matter of days if practiced regularly. We do 5 times each side for a total of 10 repetitions. Enjoy breaking a sweat.

<u>Enter the Stance:</u>   Stand on Tip Toes and bring heels out. Shift weight onto heels and turn toes out. Feet point out exactly 45 degrees making a V-shaped stance.

<u>Rooting into Earth:</u>  Bend your knees and bring weight onto the bubbling spring point. If you have weak knees you can bend less and still get a lot out of this exercise. The further you bend... the more you sweat! Whatever level you decide is comfortable to root down... it should be that you can still relax when practicing.

<u>Inhale:</u> Turn Palms out facing front. Raise hands up by bending at elbow. Forearms are level with ground.
<u>Exhale:</u> Turn hands inward for a palm-facing-palm energy connection. Feel your both relaxed and rooted.
<u>Inhale:</u> Expand the Space between palms. Adjust wrists so fingertips lead inward.
<u>Exhale:</u> Bring hands together. Adjust wrist slightly so base of hand is leading inward.
   We do 3 slow open and close movements to get used to relaxing in the posture.

**ALL IS ONE 59**

# Level-2 Qigong Form: "Drawing the Bow"

<u>Inhale Turn Left</u>: Simultaneously (1) Lift both hands *together at the same height*. Right hand ends up behind the ear like your going to throw a football. Other arm is "rounded" with palm facing palm to receive the energy of your back hand. Rounded arm has elbow lower than height of hand to assist in relaxing the arm further. (2) Shift weight over to your left leg and straighten the right leg. Do not rigidly straighten or lock the leg. It is held straight with minor effort. You will simultaneously bend your left knee bringing your weight over to the left leg. You should feel some challenge as a lot of your weight bears down on the left quadriceps.

 *Helpful Hints:* *When turning to the left... use both your legs and waist to execute the movement. Turn so that your chest is facing the same direction as your feet, which is 45 degrees. You will see that 45 degrees is the secret to this Qigong exercise.*

<u>Exhale</u>: Let the "Force of Qi" push your left hand to the posture. See the second row of photos. The first picture shows the act of sending Qi onto the left hand. *Notice that the hand receiving Qi still has not moved in the second picture.* It is allowing the Qi to "build up" before moving the hand. You can see the rest in pictures 3 and 4. It's a simple concept. When you really let the force of Qi move your hand—outside viewers will find your form looks beautiful. And you'll find that your practice has reached a higher level. This breath ends with your right palm facing your left bicep. Hands are both at the same height and fingers are all pointing in the same direction. Keep a minute bend in the elbow of your extended arm. Once in position... gaze at your index finger like a warrior.

 *Helpful Hints:* *The biggest mistake people make is to hold the receiving hand to far away. This doesn't work good because the hand needs room to move. Since the location of the receiving hand is determined during the transitions, be sure not to hold your rounded arm too far away from your body.*

# Level-2 Qigong Form: "Drawing the Bow"

<u>Inhale:</u>   Draw the Bow. Pull your right hand past your chest and then aim fingers up to the sky. Gaze at far index finger while pulling hand back.  Touch the energy as if gathering it.

<u>Exhale:</u>   Pivot from elbow arcing left hand "high up and over" to the area aligned with left knee. This is a 45 degree flip.  The middle of your chest ideally points at your hand.  Gaze at the index finger with a tiger eye. You are focused yet flowing through the Qi smoothly.

<u>Inhale:</u>   Press on Qi.  Big space between fingers.  Big Hand with thumb lowered. Ready to send Qi.  Prepare mentally as you gaze out on the horizon.

 *Helpful Hints:*  *Look at the pictures carefully.  Find the pictures where both hands are at the same height.   Your forms will be in better Qi alignment when you can remember when both hands are at the same height.*

# Level-2 Qigong Form: "Drawing the Bow"

<u>Exhale</u>: Simultaneously do the following (1) Lower Left Hand directly over left knee. It's like a slow motion karate chop leading your hand down until fingers point 45 degrees to the ground. Align hand over "center of thigh" See picture three above. (2) Lower your right (upper) hand and think about sending a "Shower of Qi" onto the lower hand. Intend your Qi to travel to the low hand. Upper hand has a gradual bend at the wrist so fingers point up. (3) While lowering feel bottom hand receiving Qi… and projecting it out the fingertips into the air. This practice will help you to externalize Qi for healing.

 *Helpful Hints:* *Eyes, Chest, Knee, Projecting Hand all line up at a 45 degree angle w/ feet. Some people don't rotate at the waist a full 45 degrees when facing either side. This leads to the chest not facing the same direction as the toes. Your body will feel a lot more Qi and be more relaxed if you can align chest hands and feet. Most people CAN do this physically however. It is more a question of awareness & attention being put onto your alignment. Also notice that both arms always have a slight bend in the elbow for roundness.*

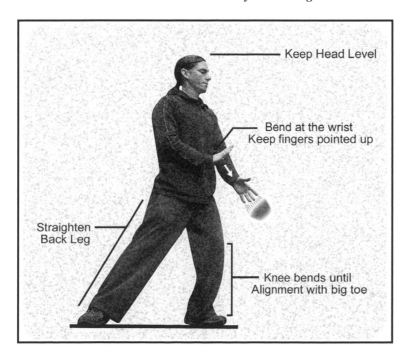

Keep Head Level

Bend at the wrist
Keep fingers pointed up

Straighten
Back Leg

Knee bends until
Alignment with big toe

# Level-2 Qigong Form: "Drawing the Bow"

<u>Inhale</u>: Draw top hand up close to body at a 45 degree angle.  When at the top "open" your palm slightly more.

<u>Exhale</u>: Down in a straight line on the inside lane.  Arc out to the side and back up on the outside lane.
Send Qi from 1 hand to the other. Then project out your lower hand into the air. 3 extra large spirals.

**Helpful Hints:** *Look at the pictures above.   The lower hand always has palm facing the
same direction as the inner thigh.  This is another key alignment.  The upper
hand is considerably bent at the wrist. Notice the "L-shape" this creates.
Your hands are "Boxing In" Qi making it project with far greater strength.*

<u>Inhale</u>: Transition to the other side by turning lower palm up to greet upper hand.  With a twist of the wrist...
change weight to other leg.  Lift hands in a gradual manner "sloping upwards" timing hands to arrive
in the push hands posture once fully rotated to the other side.  For extra credit you can "Pull the Qi"
as you change sides while lifting hands. This adds another dimension of Qi & beauty to your practice.

**Helpful Hints:** *Transitioning gracefully from one side to the other can be a learning process. See pictures
from left to right.  Notice that as I cross the center both knees are equally bent.  Then as I
bear weight on the opposite thigh my back leg becomes straight.  Knee bends to align to
the big toe, but no farther.  Knee should never pass the big toe.*

<u>Exiting Drawing the Bow</u>: After performing 5 repetitions on each side for a total of 10 projections...
Inhale come to center.  Exhale lower hands and rise off bent knee.

# Level-2 Qigong Healing Form: "Full-Body Spiraling"

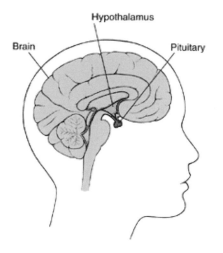

Full-Body Spiraling helps the endocrine system, your facial appearance, eyes and clarity of mind. There is an increase in microcirculation to the brain as the practitioner gently spirals his or her body focusing on finger tips passing through Qi. As the spiraling becomes more minute & less physical the energy becomes greater leading the spiraling automatically. Simply focus on the pulsation of Qi in the hands and imagine it is being sent to the pituitary gland inside the brain. The hands are held in prayer hands posture with the base of the thumbs against the eyebrow center. After a few minutes of spiraling, slowly open hands and cover the eyes. Feel the warmth entering the eyes and imagine bright lights entering the eyes. Massage the face without lifting hands more than a few millimeters off the skin's surface. Massage circularly for one minute. Then lower hands down into prayer posture at the chest center and down into closing.

# Level-2 Qigong Healing Form: "Nine-Breath Method"

In ancient times, the Chinese did not separate the notion of Qi from the notion of Breath. The most ancient Chinese character for the word "Qi" has been compared to that of 'Vapors' rising up like steam. They held the belief that breath was inseparable from Qi, therefore it would be correct to say that "Fresh Air" is the Qi itself and that the mind is the computer that governs and directs it. Through conscious breathing we can perform & experience a heightened state of alertness & connection to the universe. This is very useful for many reasons. Often times we feel weighed down by the pressures of life. Nine-Breath to the rescue.

E-motions *(energy in motion)* determine the flow of Qi & consequentially our health. Lots of our students find that this particular exercise helps to "break out" of a low time. When a person is sad or feels weakened for whatever reason, it is like a thick shell that blocks their flow of Qi. Perhaps counseling isn't enough to break the shell—try Qigong.

Modern     Ancient

## *What does the Nine-Breath Method feel like?*

Many people are spiritually moved by the energy of this practice. When performed correctly, the entire body is ecstatic and pulsating with blood and Qi. An "electrical wave" pulses down the legs. The Navel area where the hands are kept gets very warm and the biological sensation is pleasurable. Sometimes sweat appears over the navel instantly. After proficiency in the technique is gained, people feel their energy expand outward beyond the body. It is the ultimate connection with the non-physical spirit self.

When your body begins to physically vibrate from the inside you can easily perceive life beyond the veil of illusion. Things are no longer solid. Many people will see this energy with their eyes open. It looks like blue vapors rising like steam. When I do the practice my body begins humming softly and gently sways from side to side. In that moment I experience a bliss, which is common with this technique. My first thought is to smile and thank God for this wisdom. All life challenges seem unimportant for the moment. My mind is automatically drawn to "The Source". As I do more sets of the exercise this Qi becomes so powerful that I feel one with the Earth below me. And this level of Qi is not unique to me. Many thousands of people have learned this practice with similar results.

## *Expectations and Reality*

A few people will not feel a lot in the beginning. Most people however do. Sometimes it takes patience and practice, but usually after doing in in Level-2 and Level-3 for two days the person gets the idea. However, some of our best instructors took several weeks before they really "got it". They would later come to me and say something like, "I did not understand why everyone around me was having such a powerful experience with this exercise... and then I did the Tumo breathing a slightly different way and it felt like a "spiritual energy bomb" went off in my abdomen. I think now I understand the technique."

## *Safety Precautions with Nine-Breath Method*

There are a few people that get light headed from this practice. After teaching Nine-Breath Method to thousands of people, we know the exercise is safe. The only risk factor is taking too much air & getting light headed. If you feel disoriented during it... simply breathe softer, which controls the lightheadedness. You simply govern the amount of air you take in. If you have the tendency towards lightheadedness it may be that your constitution is weak. Always practice sitting in these cases and breathe softer.

# Nine-Breath Method Helpful Suggestions

## *Slowing Down Your Breathing*

High Level Qigong Practitioners can dramatically slow down their heart rate by slowing down their breathing. Prolonging the *length of each breath* also slows down the mind activity and creates a highly aware state of meditation. It is therefore a good observation to note that your breathing patterns will affect your heart rate, mind, and other physiological functions. During the Nine Warrior Breaths there is a tendency to breathe fast & furious, but this is not correct. We desire to take FULL inhales with a smooth tempo. On the last 2 breaths we slow down the breathing a lot to prepare for the breath lock and sink down. The ninth breath is taken exceptionally deep and slow so that we are not in a rush to inhale right away. At the core of the practice is a long prolonged exhale. Sometimes I will exhale for over 1 minute. This is only possible by slowing down the last inhale and relaxing.

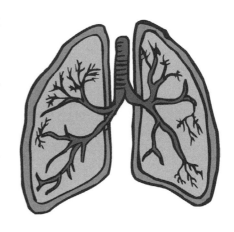

## *Relax Your Back & Shoulders*

The Warriors Breath and Breath Lock have a tendency to lock up the muscles in the upper back and shoulders. When you reach the top of the ninth breath think about relaxing. When you sink down the air to the lower abdomen you use a gentle "abdominal manipulation" to pressurize the Qi. Often times people will tighten up their entire body and this is undesirable. Tightness will stop the Qi in its tracks. The main area people will tighten is the upper back & shoulders. Now that you know... take extra care to relax through it all.

## *Lower Jaw During the Ninth Exhale*

We touch the tip of our tongue to the Lower Palate while exhaling. In addition, the Qi will be much stronger if you gently relax your jaw and purse your lips while exhaling. *To relax the jaw, we think about it loosening and being lowered slightly down and forward.* When your JAW is relaxed then your whole body will be relaxed. It is common knowledge in hypnotherapy circles that the Jaw is a holding place of a master relaxation switch. If you can successfully relax the muscles of your Jaw the entire practice will be enhanced considerably.

# Tumo Breathing Concepts

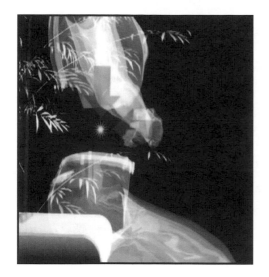

*The signs of successful Tumo include: Feeling like you can exhale for a really long time, warmth & humming that pervades your entire body, strong pulsation in hands, naval & profound feelings of Gratitude.*

The term Tumo comes from Tibet. It means Inner Fire and often is used to describe the Heat Generation exercises practiced by the Himalayan monks. In Tibet there is a tradition of drying out wet towels in the nude. Discovery Channel did a special on this and indeed the footage was spectacular. You can see steam rising from their backs as they "steam" the towels dry. But what is Tumo Breathing? Many will give different answers. For our system of Qigong, Tumo defines a type of gentle abdominal manipulation that greatly boosts circulation of internal energy. By saying "internal energy" we mean that it boosts circulation of energy that exists already inside you. In nine-breath method we take "external energy" from the warriors breath and then make it our own "internal". Tumo breathing takes this newly acquired Qi and puts it under "gentle pressurization" to increase the power of its circulation. Just as a shower with more water pressure is moving water more effectively, the Tumo breath gently increases the circulation of internal energy in the body.

Tumo breathing can be done on its own, but its effects are much more noticeable when performed within the Nine-Breath Method. During a normal exhale, the abdomen will deflate and lose its size. **In Tumo, we are creating a specific shape for the abdomen while performing the exhale. We breathe out through pursed lips to help us exhale for a longer time period.**

Version A: The abdomen is "gently held out & down" with abdominal muscles slightly harder. It actually takes on the rounded appearance as in photo A. This is of course simpler than version B. Some like A better and some like B better. Both versions have a different feel and both are awesome. We like to interchange between the two versions frequently and this will greatly accelerate your understanding.

Version B: After dropping the air down into our abdomen, we "pull in" our pliable & completely relaxed abdomen towards the spine. **The key is that one does not tighten the abdomen until placement is back inwards. After abdomen has been pulled in THEN gently tighten & contract the abdomen.** It may take sometime before "effortlessness" will be possible. After the abdomen has been pulled back you gently press down... then softly pull back... then down again. Its like stairs. The movements are very subtle and if you are straining your missing the boat.

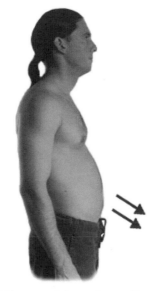

**Tumo Version A**

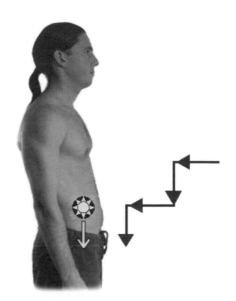

**Tumo Version B**

# Nine Breath Method Complete Instructions

The main focus is to successfully perform Nine-Breath Method whenever you want to, both in the Level-2 form and on its own. Getting it right takes some relaxation skill. We will strive to relax while doing a mildly intense practice. In order to be successful it helps to learn each individual component separately. (1) Warrior's Breath (2) Breath Lock & Sink Down (3) Tumo Exhale Version A & B

## Stage 1: Nine Consecutive Warrior Breaths

**9 Warrior Breaths:**
All the Way In – All the Way Out

Use entire lung capacity. Breathe into the <u>chest</u> area deeply. Shoulders will rise and fall. It should make a loud sound through the nostrils as the air comes in. This process is an ion exchange and releases old stale air from the body. We like to gently lean back on the inhale and gently lean forward on the exhale. It is a way to infuse the body with large amounts of Oxygen and Qi. On its own the warriors breath is a low level practice. When it is combined with stage 2 and 3 it reaches its potential. Use your body to move gently with each breath. Do not forcefully breathe. On the 8th breath begin to go slower and deeper.

**Breath Lock:** for 1-3 seconds. Then
Sink Air Downward into Abdomen

## Stage 2: Breath Lock and Sink Air Down

At the top of the ninth breath we perform a short 1-3 second breath lock. This gives more time for our lungs to absorb the Qi from the air. During the Breath lock the first thing you do while holding the air is "relax your shoulders". After the breath lock, we **sink** the air from your chest down into the abdomen. This is when the magic will happen instantly. The main key for success is to drop the air into a **pliable/completely relaxed abdomen**. Its 100% without strain & has a round shape. Like Buddha Belly.

## Stage 3: Tumo Prolonged Exhale

The Tumo uses gentle abdominal manipulation to maximize the circulation of Qi in the body. *Pictures are showing the abdomen for you to view what is mechanically happening, however hands will be covering navel center.* There are 2 variations of the method, because we find both to be extremely valuable. Version A is simpler and involves gently pressing out and down while exhaling. For some people they will prefer the simplicity. Version B is slightly different. Upon dropping air down, we pull a completely relaxed abdomen backwards towards the spine. Then we gently contract down & back...subtly alternating down & back.

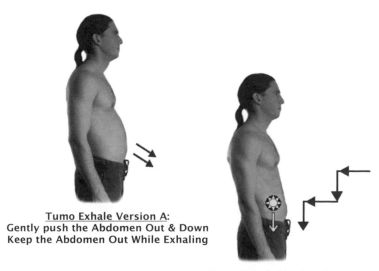

**Tumo Exhale Version A:**
Gently push the Abdomen Out & Down
Keep the Abdomen Out While Exhaling

**Tumo Exhale Version B:**
Pull *Relaxed* Abdomen Inward to Spine
Alternate Pressing In & Down like Stairs

# Level-3 Workshop
## *Wuji Style Qigong & Nine-Breath Healing*

# Level-3 Intro: Formless Wuji Style Qigong

<u>Wuji Defined</u>: Formless and undifferentiated.   Beyond polarity and gender.
Taoism says: From the emptiness of Wuji (one) came Taiji yin/yang (two).
From Taiji came the ten thousand things (everything in existence).

Returning to innocence and no-mind is what Wuji Style Qigong is all about.   Sometimes you just want to play like a child in the leaves.  Wuji is for moments like these, yet it never replaces standing forms. *Wuji is best used as the "icing on the cake" after you've done either the Level-1 or 2 Qigong form.*

Wuji is the "gateway" to a Master Level practitioner's understanding of manipulating & strengthening the human energy field.  Wuji means formless and therefore, practicing Wuji Style Qigong has no actual form.  Therefore, one must ask, "Is it a free for all?  Can you go and do whatever you want?" Basically yes, however there are certain movements that will assist in making the Wuji experience more powerful.  Using our system of **7 Wuji Style Movements** you can master the Wuji style and enter the "Qigong Gate" (metaphor for really understanding the nature of Qi). Learning these seven movements & their subtleties will elevate your understanding of Qi tremendously.

When we are practicing Qigong forms and exercises, we're cultivating in Taiji.  Breathe in here... move this way there... it has a right way and wrong way.  This is Yin and Yang—or duality consciousness.  In Wuji, we are returning to the undifferentiated source where there is "no right or wrong movements". It is a completely different way of practicing, since there is no set form.

## How to use this System

My original intention for designing a third level was to allow people the opportunity to practice the way I did when I was alone. For years I had loved the Wuji Style ways, but I noticed that it was very difficult to teach. *Wuji Style will draw on a person's previous knowledge of Qigong & Tai Chi.* I had seen other Qigong Masters teaching Free Form Wuji Style Qigong, but without any real instruction on how to make the movements. (The students would just sort of float around) The more Qigong you know the better. Of course when the master performs Wuji Style Qigong it looks beautiful and powerful! That's because Wuji is spontaneously drawing from your databank of Qigong.

The 3rd level originally took thousands of hours and years to design. I gave my best effort to explain the important Qigong principles and movements a person would need for having a successful and powerful Wuji experience. We called these principles **Seven Wuji Style Movements**. Within Qigong there are thousands of styles and none of the Qigong forms I've ever seen are identical. After seeing so many different kinds of Qigong, I noticed ALL Qigong movements have common attributes and while it appeared that these different forms were so different they were often using variations of *Seven Wuji movements.* Knowing these 7 "Broad Classifications" of Qigong movements & the precise laws behind them is equal to knowing 7000 possible movements! Once you get it... you're sure to have the "Ah-ha! Moment" when you realize your having more fun than you thought possible.

## Wuji Stepping & Staying Rooted

*Walking without waking up the guards*

The goal is to move gracefully with poise and precision through the energy plasma in the air. We accomplish this by specialized walking. Of course, you can just float around and walk however you want! Or you could practice like a Qigong master. Obviously precision is a good thing here. So lets discuss how to walk when in Wuji.

Begin with knees slightly bent. Ideally you will keep your head at the same level the entire practice without bobbing up and down. Stepping forward is like gliding through the air. Feel Qi around you. Walk like a stealth ninja making the least impact on the ground as possible. In Qigong, this is known as "walking on eggshells".

1) Leading foot lands with heel touching ground first
2) Then bend knee as you carefully plant the rest of your foot down
3) Glide forward without raising your head higher or lower
4) Bring your weight directly over the "bubbling well" point
5) You aim to be totally rooted over that foot before lifting back leg

# Category #1: Subtle Movements

There are 4 subtle movements in our system of Qigong: Spiraling, Pulsing, Pressing and Rotating. You have been using the first three a lot already in Level-1 & 2 and now we are learning to use them in Wuji practice. When we are moving our body during the Wuji practice we can spiral often. It is used in a gesture that brings Qi towards your body. *The key to using spiraling successfully lies in making smaller and smaller spirals until it cannot be seen easily.* Then we use the spiral to press on the Qi, which is even more subtle. *Spiraling is always followed by pressing.* After you press on Qi you can move again—pressing on Qi everywhere you move.

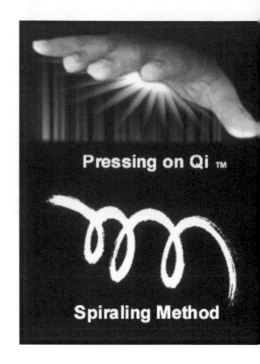

**Pressing on Qi** ™

**Spiraling Method**

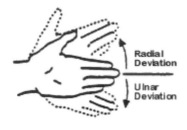

Radial Deviation

Ulnar Deviation

Rotating at the Wrists is the 4th subtle movement and can be tricky for some people. It is easier when we isolate the forearm with one hand and make a movement up & down like in the left photo. As you get more advanced in Qigong you will see that this becomes a very important movement to know.

## *Spiraling & Rotating Combined is Double the Power*

While you are performing the spiraling technique you can rotate the wrists at the same time. Begin rotating the wrists **straight up & down.** Move less & less until the movement is a "Micro-Movement". It should be almost undetectable to the eye. When you do the rotating palms and the spiraling you are harnessing Qi from a greater surface area of your hand and you will notice the Qi double or triple.

## *Putting a Spin on the Energy*

The Magnetic Energy within our surrounding environment responds to being "patted on" like a baby. You've already seen that with pulsing, the lighter and more precise the pulse, the stronger it is. This magnetic sensation can become powerful enough to generate heat in the hand over 112 degrees. What is the secret to amplifying the magnetic sensation and thus the energy? One of them is to put a "spin on the energy". This occurs when we micro spiral-rotate in all our Qigong, especially Wuji. Below the picture exaggerates the size of the movement and helps you to learn. After you own the method yourself it will be invisible to others eyes because it is so small. It becomes second nature.

**Bending at Wrist While Spiraling Maximizes the Hand's Surface Area putting "Spin" on the Qi**

**Rotating Absorbs Qi From the Normally Unused Radial & Ulnar Surface**

**Until Now...
You've used only the Palm's Surface to absorb Qi in Spiraling**

# Category #2: Ball Making Movements

*Spherical Open & Close Movements that are Palm-facing-Palm*

Energy can be strengthened by containing it inside a sphere. In fact, the Universe itself is spherical. The key is to "contain the energy" by holding a palm-facing-palm energy connection. To begin Wuji we will start with several open & close movements before taking our first step forward. When you step simultaneously make a sphere like in the upper left photo. Shoulders are relaxed and head is level. Walking around slowly "carve" a sphere of energy into the air. Rotate your hands so now opposite hand is on top. Further shape and fortify the ball by **pressing inward** on the Qi while changing hands.

Primary Identifying Trait of Ball Movements: "Palm-Facing-Palm"

Start Moving! Get Creative! Perform smaller and then larger spherical movements. Move around with **very slow big steps.** We can make a bigger sized ball to create more Qi. The more distance—the more Qi will fill it. Continue rotating and counter Rotating circularly. Feel the Qi all over your arms now. Breath in... expand hands for a bigger ball... exhale and bring the ball inward smaller.

# Category #3: Projection Style Movements

*Sending from 1 Palm to Another... Then out into Surrounding Air*

For me the projection style movement carries more power than any other type of movement in Qigong. That is saying a lot. Drawing the bow gets you familiar with how it works. You can aim high into the sky and then exhale while lowering both hands. You're training Mind Intention. Use one hand to send energy to the other. *The far hand is emitting double Qi, which is why I like it so much.* As you move around send Qi to one of your hands. This really opens your meridians and heats up your entire body. You will feel double Qi emitting from the projecting hand. MicroSpiral/Rotate the upper hand.

## Project & Receive Alternating Movements

Beautiful to see and powerful to practice is a circular combination of the projecting & drawing movements. Receiving is performed by holding one arm far away with palm facing at you 45 degrees and the other arm with fingers pointing directly at the hand 45 degrees. This posture is very round and that is what gives it power. It's a state of consciousness that we enter where we receive the blessing.

For this method we are projecting and receiving from both hands.
Make a "Receiving Gesture" on the inhale – draw in Qi.
Make a "Sending Gesture" on the exhale – project out Qi.

# Category #4: Push Hands Style Movements

*Sending from 1 Palm to Another… "Catching Energy" to Assist Movement*

These movements are wonderful for blood circulation and similar to the projection style movements on the previous page. The main difference is that instead of 'projecting' it from the receiving hand out into the air you're **Catching the Energy** and allowing it to 'push' the receiving hand and assist in your movement. All of the push hands movements are extremely valuable in the Wuji Style Qigong. *At certain times… you can MicroSpiral/Rotate the sending hand to increase the Qi.*

In addition to the **Palm-Facing-Palm push hands movements** you're familiar with from Level-1 and 2 forms, it is also possible to perform an **Energy Intended push hands movement** whereby you can catch the Force of Qi without aiming palm facing-palm. See images above. Using mind, the practitioner projects a beam of Qi outward and INTENDS it to arc around back catching it in the other hand. People are always amazed at how strong the Qi force is simply intending, no longer needing to aim. Inhale and do nothing. Exhale, transmitting hand moves forward. Receiving hand gets pushed back.

*To further understand the properties of this special movement, imagine holding an "energy slinky" each end touching palms. Lift one hand higher than the other - think about that hand sending the slinky (energy) over to the other hand. You will feel this pushes Qi down onto the hand even though the palms are not facing. You can feel that it creates an arc shaped energy flow. In other words—Qi does not only move linearly—it moves in arcs also. Use this understanding.*

This is a very powerful type of movement and uses the same pattern as the steel bar on the front wheels of a train. As in other movements, your pattern takes on an oval shape. You can look at this method as a bigger version of the spiraling method. Recall that Standing Wuji Style and Qigong Walking are done with a continuous flow. Therefore, one is not limited to using the Locomotive style movements only in front of the body. You can turn to the sides, bend down, or use them over your head. This is another one of the most powerful movements and I believe that is because Qi likes to move in spiral patterns.

As your moving, one hand is up while the other is below. One hand is close to your body while the other one is away. Thus, palm facing palm doesn't occur, however you must consciously "attune" the energy from both palms to each other. You will sense a tornado-like strand of energy linking the palms even though they are not facing each other. Also, as in the other movements, you can sometimes pause the movement and pulse the hands using the Spiraling & Rotating pulsing hands method. The hallmark feature of the Locomotive style movement is the hands always being held 180 degrees across from each other.

## *The Master Transition Movement*

Graceful transition between each movement is the key in Wuji. Being that is the case you'll want to learn to connect different movements into one singular flow. **The Locomotive movement is the ultimate connecting and transitioning movement.** Going from Locomotive style movements to push hand style movements is an especially powerful favorite of mine. The main premise of a True Wuji Style Qigong is to be smooth, continuous and be able to use various moves interchangeably without sudden jerkiness in the fluidity. The locomotive always serves in this capacity.

# Category #6: Cleansing Style Movements

*Palm is Angled 45 Degrees towards body. Downward Washing Motion.*

We use this type of movement in Full-Body Cleansing and it is a rather common type of movement in Qigong. When it is done properly the hand is held at 45 degrees along the body to create the strongest movement of Qi. Here's how it works. You may be doing a projection style movement and then gracefully transition into a locomotive move. Then your left hand might slowly glide down your body at 45 degrees as you intend energy from the top downward. The movements are done as if we are "cleaning ourselves" and it is that intention that counts. Sometimes it is done as a gesture to move stagnant Qi. *It is also known as a Cleansing Style Movements. Many Qigong forms use this movement over particular trouble organs or joints.* They employ visualization or intention to amplify the effect. The rule of thumb for all cleansing movements is that during the inhale you are "preparing" to do it. On the exhale you are making the downward slow cleansing movement.

# Category #7: Swimming Style Movements

*Slowly Swimming through the Qi Plasma All Around*

We saved the strangest movement for last!  Yes, while it looks silly...you can bet your going to like it. After learning all the other movements, this one really shows you that the Qi truly is everywhere and that it can be "tapped into" in just about every move.  **The Swimming Style Movements are a lot like the locomotive movements in that "one arm is up while another is down".**  You bring your shoulders into the motions.  People always laugh when doing this one and that's because they feel so much Qi!

Bring your awareness to slowing down as if swimming through the Water (Qi) and when you lower your hands— its as if you are passing your whole arm through the Qi and pressing on Qi.  *The waist and shoulders can and should both be involved in the motions.*  It allows for a real opening of the hips and shoulders.  Think about the Qi all around you as you move through the air.

## *Full Body Pressing*

This concept is the DEEPEST most powerful connection one can experience in Wuji.  So far you've pressed on Qi with your hands and arms.  Now we move to learn how to press on Qi with your entire body!!  No other movement helps you learn the concept like swimming

Begin swimming and pause in a posture similar to the left image.  Pulse your entire body back and forth and FEEL the Qi on your midsection.  Without stepping rotate left or right from your waist keeping arms fixed. Press inward on Qi between arms and think about energy being absorbed by your chest and abdomen. Slowly swim with this awareness.  Use waist rotation and hold arms fixed pressing inwards.  Very powerful.

# Advanced Nine-Breath Method

## *Tumo Versions C & D*

# Advanced Nine-Breath Method Series

## Global Healing Meditation
## Gentle Kundalini Activation
## Hands on Healing for Others

Students undertaking the Advanced Versions of Nine-Breath Method are required to have practiced the easier versions FIRST for several hours. After a moderate level of comprehension with easier versions has been attained... it's alright to proceed with Advanced Applications.

The advanced versions of 9BM use **Prolonged Sublimation and Retention Times** during the practice. This considerably enhance the power of this method. People undertaking these exercises are required to remain aware of their tendency to become lightheaded.

It is easy to establish the body's sensitivity by starting out with softer warrior breaths and gradually progressing into louder ones. The rule of thumb is that when you feel LIGHTHEADED make the breath have less sound. If you want to feel the energy STRONGER make the sound of the inhale a little bit louder. Because SOUND OF BREATH is easy to control... we teach that the practice is safe.

In addition to longer hold times & sublimation without air in the lungs, the more advanced versions of Nine-Breath Method use sequences of Warrior Breaths beyond the standard 9. We use 18, 27 and even 36 Warrior Breaths before initiating the later stages of the technique. Adding this increased level of Qi and Oxygen to your bloodstream before beginning a long hold or sublimation without air really gets the motor running. However, its imperative that the "Lightheaded-Group" of people pace themselves before taking off running to the races. If a person gets dizzy from 9 warrior breaths... for sure 18 will be more intense. Yet, if the student simply is aware of their tendency even the most sensitive and light-headed prone individuals can proceed safely by making the 18 breaths or the 27 breaths <u>more quiet</u> than they would 9 breaths.

During these GUIDED MEDIATIONS using Advanced Nine-Breath Method it is IMPOSSIBLE for me to pick perfect breath timing for everyone. For example: My voice may be saying "HOLD", but YOUR BODY might be saying PLEASE BREATHE OUT NOW!!! It is obvious that you should not press too far beyond your comfort zone. Ignore instructions and breathe in or out SOONER until you are capable to follow the guidance in the Meditation.

For this Audio CD I have chosen Sublimation and Inhale Hold Times with a great deal of thought and planning. These hold times are realistic for most, but they can push some to be uncomfortable *if their lungs are not strong enough.* With time... your body should be able to ADAPT to the practice... and EVOLVE into greater hold times without discomfort. Until then please FOLLOW BREATH TIMING THAT FEELS NATURAL FOR YOU. *You can still maintain the visualizations while following your own natural breathing rhythms.*

# Advanced Nine-Breath Method  Version C
## <u>The Prolonged Retention of Breath</u>

Version C is similar to the easier Level-2 practices.  The difference is that the inhale is held for longer and we often use sequences of either 9, 18 or 27 warrior breaths before performing the breath hold.

During the various meditations and hands on healing applications, Version C's method will differ slightly, but the technique itself is the same for any application.   So lets begin with an understanding behind the structure of the technique so that when you hear the Guided Meditation you will be free from thinking about the technical aspects and better able to focus on the visualizations.

Step 1:   Take Nine, Eighteen or Twenty Seven Warrior Breaths.
Depending on your tolerance level you can make these louder or quitter.   Then...

Step 2:   Slow down on the last breath... and Fully Inhale.   HOLD.  You'll probably be tense at first.
Immediately release a very small amount of air to help you relax and hold longer.
This short release of pressure helps during LONG Retention times.
*** You will continue to hold for 15-60 seconds based on your comfort level.

Step 3:   During this HOLD we'll softly bring in some TUMO.
Effortlessly draw abdominal wall **IN 1 INCH** towards spine.  Belly is soft when you do this.
You will feel a pleasurable pulsation in your abdomen if you do this right.

Step 4:   Exhale slowly out pursed lips.   This exhale may occur faster than your exhale
on the easier versions of Nine-Breath Method.   After holding for 40 seconds you
may feel like Huffing all your air out and frantically breathing in and out again.

Try to breathe out slower following retentions, but be aware the tendency is
for most people...  after a long retention...  that they have to breathe out sooner.

*Find the middle path.
*As long as you exhale without a sound others could hear... you're doing good.
*With time... you will get to higher states of relaxation through the exhale.

Step 5:   Circulate the energy with DEEP QUIET ABDOMINAL BREATHING

***   This is a key point..  And for people that finish a breath sequence early because they
can't hold or exhale for as long as the GUIDED MEDITATION calls for they should always
revert back to this DEEP QUIET ABDOMINAL BREATHING in between sets.

Sometimes the best part of the practice is performing the visualizations and simply doing
the DEEP QUIET ABDOMINAL BREATHING inbetween sets.

*The Ice Man a.k.a. Wim Hof
showed us the power of sublimation.*

# Advanced Nine-Breath Method  Version D
# The Prolonged Sublimation of Breath

Version D is profound... it truly teaches us what the "Breathless State" is like since we go for long periods without any air in the body at all. This lack of air helps us to fully relax... far beyond what is possible on a retention hold. When people empty their lungs & "hang out" in the **empty air state** it can be the most quiet space advanced meditators ever find themselves.  We often use sequences of either 9, 18, 27 & even 36 warrior breaths before performing the breath hold.  The major difference with Version D is that the HOLD at the end of the warrior breaths is much shorter.  Only 3 seconds.  Then a full breath out of all the air leaves a ripple of pleasurable waves pulsing from the Dan Tien.

We say BREATHE ALL YOU'RE AIR OUT IN 2 SECONDS.   This is a mildly forceful breath to quickly  expel the air.  However... do not attempt to take out every last bit of air from your lungs.  We say breathe out 95% of your air.   Save 5% so you can relax easier. During the guided meditations and hands on healing applications, Version D's method will differ slightly, but the technique itself is the same for any application.  So lets begin with an understanding behind the structure of the technique so when you hear the Guided Meditation you will be free from thinking about the technical aspects.

Step 1:  Take Nine, Eighteen, Twenty Seven or Thirty Six Warrior Breaths.
  Depending on your tolerance level you can make these louder or quitter. Then...

Step 2:  Slow down on the last breath... and Fully Inhale.   HOLD.  For about 3 seconds.
  Then release all your air... breathing semi forcefully out your lips.
   *Remember not to breath every last ounce of air out.  Only 95%
   *If you feel uncomfortable after exhaling... sip a little bit of air to take the edge off.

Step 3:  This "Empty Air State" we call sublimation.  Going without air.
  You'll be HOLDING without air in the sublimation... Yet you'll be TOTALLY RELAXED.
  Focus will either be in the Dan Tien and Solar Plexus Region... or...
  The Perineum, between the genitals and anus... depending on which mediation your doing.

  Bring in some TUMO and effortlessly draw abdominal wall **IN 1 INCH** towards spine.
  Belly is soft when you do this.  You will feel a pleasurable pulsation in your abdomen
  if you do this right.   Depending on how many warrior breaths we take beforehand
  we sublimate without air anywhere from 45 to 90 seconds on the Meditation CD's.

   *Some people will need to inhale sooner than others.
   *Follow your body's wisdom.  Going a few seconds longer is ok but don't push too hard.
   *Most people can handle the SUBLIMATION TIMES on the Meditation CD's, however
    Following your own natural rhythm is critical as it would be impossible to create a
    Practice CD where everyone is at the same level.

With time... your body should be able to ADAPT to the practice... and EVOLVE into greater hold times without discomfort.   Until then please FOLLOW BREATH TIMING THAT FEELS NATURAL FOR YOU. *You can still maintain the visualizations while following your own natural breathing rhythms.*

Step 4:  Inhale BIG, WITH LOUD SOUND, sitting up perfectly straight, drawing Qi up your back
  to either your Lotus Crown or Your Eyebrow Center... depending on which meditation your
  doing.   This hold is only for 15-30 seconds.  It is here that you may find yourself having
  SUDDEN ENLIGHTENMENT.   You may see lights behind closed eyes.  Gently Contract the
  abdominal muscles inward slightly with a slight amount of effort.  Really it is effortless.

Step 5:  Long exhale breathing out pursed lips... Try to keep it slow and quiet.
Step 6:  Circulate the energy with DEEP QUIET ABDOMINAL BREATHING

# Advanced Nine-Breath Method Series
# <u>Global Healing Meditation</u>

Next to being inside a two-thousand-person 9-Breath Circle, the global healing meditation is the next best thing. After versions A, B, C & D of the Nine-Breath Method have been moderately understood students can progress into more enjoyable meditations like this one and the *Gentle Kundalini Activation* practice taught in the Level-4 seminar. These advanced meditations saturate the body with oxygen & energy. This helps to fight inflammation, harmful bacteria, cancer... and quickly eliminate stress. In fact, I have had the deepest spiritual moments of my entire life using the advanced nine-breath method in meditation.

On a biological level, the Global Healing Meditation directs MIND attention into the Navel & Solar Plexus areas. In the presence of such profound energy... when our mind attention goes to the abdomen it brings Qi to this region. Energy follows mind and so the practice is nourishing lower vital organs.

On a spiritual level we are IN SERVICE... Healing the Planet and Specific People we love. We use the visualization of the EARTH in the Dan Tien and Solar Plexus Region. The energy received from this practice not only HEALS our body cells... it heals humanity & the Earth. The structure of the Advanced 9-Breath Method Global Healing Meditation is separated into 7 actual rounds of breathing:

Rounds 1-3:   Version C with the PROLONGED RETENTION.
Rounds 4-7:   Version D with the PROLONGED SUBLIMATION.
And with each round the number of Warrior Breaths increases by 9.

During the first 3 sets, which utilize Prolonged Retention...
You'll start out with 9 Warrior Breaths... then 18... and then progress to 27.
*As stated previously, people who get light headed can cut back the sound of breaths.

The 4th set begins the Prolonged Sublimation...
You'll start out with 9 Warrior Breaths... then 18... then 27... *and with Retention we finish with 36.*

<u>The First 3 Sets</u>: have a long HOLD time on the 9th, 18th or 27th Inhale.
This is a special time in the Global Healing Meditation where we prepare our transmission.
We conjure up FEELINGS of PEACE while absorbing the energy.
While continuing to hold we envision our intended recipient of Qi... the whole planet Earth.

Inside we become EMPOWERED and yet HUMBLE and the same time.
During the Long Tumo Exhale we breathe out blessings onto the Earth.
It feels wonderful. We share the GOOD FEELINGS we are generating with HUMANITY.

**When your listening to the Mediation CD you'll probably be finished exhaling without guidance acknowledging it. With everyone's different breath timing... the Meditation assumes you will go into DEEP ABDOMINAL BREATHING once you've finished a sequence. Continue to hold the visualization you are hearing about while waiting to guided into the next series of warrior breaths.

# Advanced Nine-Breath Method
## Global Healing Meditation

The Last 4 Sets: Have a long SUBLIMATION time on the 9th, 18th, 27th and 36th Exhale.  This is a special time in the Global Healing Meditation where we COUNT PULSATIONS & TOTALLY RELAX.  We visualize the EARTH as the focal point in the NAVEL SOLAR PLEXUS region.  With almost no air in your body you'll be totally relaxed. COUNT PULSATIONS even though you may wander off the correct number.

When your counting pulsations, if you forget where you are just select another number & begin counting there.  Counting serves to hold your focus on the pulsation and helps increase energy.  If you do not enjoy the practice of counting feel free to eliminate this part of the practice.  For me personally, I like the counting.  It makes the energy much stronger for me.  Can we count without being overly rigid?  Sure!  Just do the counting from an OBSERVER standpoint.  During the meditation I send gentle reminders that we aren't MAKING this process happen.  Rather we observe it happen.  **Allowing** the process to happen.  Practice like a 7 year old child.   So goes the teaching.

Visualize at the point of pulsation our intended recipient of Qi, which is the planet Earth or specific person we wish to send healing to.   There will occur a pulsation in the abdomen.  You'll hold the image there.

During the LOUD INHALE that follows after SUBLIMATION we draw energy UP OUR SPINE, over head and hold the vision of the Earth (or our person being Healed) at the Eye Brow Center.  We RELAX into this breath hold for about 20-30 seconds and generate feelings of PEACE and LOVE.

The long exhale is awesome.  We breathe out blessings onto Earth or the person we are send healing to.  In between sets we revert to the DEEP QUIET ABDOMINAL BREATHING.  The last round is a gratitude and abundance breath. It directs our love back to the TRUE SOURCE.  When the meditation ends our body cells are vibrating with a greater connection to ALL THAT IS.

# Qi Transmission, Prayer and Healing

The art of transferring Vital Energy to another human being is taught across all cultures and all religions. Every society across the world has different terms & mechanics for this process. Before the 1950's and the slow inception of Eastern thought to the West, most Westerners only had Prayer as their means of "Qi Transmission". Prayer focuses our intention, which alone is the most powerful thing. The church has reported countless miraculous healings that occur through the physical body of one being to another. As a Qigong practitioner. You'll soon realize the skills to tap into this source (or you may already know). *But there are rules in the SSQ system for Qi Transmission.* My mentors have all said, "Make yourself healthy first before taking up healing. Your personal vitality as a healer is the key."

## *Picking Up Others Stuff is Optional — But it Happens*

There are many approaches to healing. To name a few: Acupuncture, Chiropractic, Massage Therapy, Nurses, Surgeons, Doctors, Mental Health Specialists etc. All of these practices have *the potential* to harm the healer. Many doctors have health problems because they are absorbing the negative energy from too many clients. Anyone in health care is dealing with this (whether they are aware of it or not).

A person looking to give Qi to another person (healing) needs to use Universal Energy, not their own supply. Many forms of healing claim their method is safe—and I believe there are some methods which are safer than others, but I have seen too many healers in an unhealthy state from literally absorbing the identical ailments of their clients. Granted these are people who see 'lots' of clients. *Therefore, It is best to reserve sending Qi for immediate family until you are stronger. This is the first rule in our system. Of course, you are going to learn Nine-Breath Method Qi Transmission and be tempted to use it often. It is so powerful, yet I have given you my warning that this is not for the faint of heart and that it should be used exclusively for loved ones and relatives until your capacity as a healer is more developed.*

The average 'career life' of a massage therapist is short. They often have high energy in the beginning, but often get horrible pain in their hands and other areas. Many have to stop their practice and they mistakenly believe that it was because they 'used their hands too much'. The tension they took out of their clients went into their hands. It's not only massage therapists - its doctors, nurses, psychologists and all health care service men/woman. Many studies have shown Heart specialists often end up with heart problems themselves. Lung specialists often get lung problems. This is statistical information and indeed too strange to be coincidence. Psychologists typically get depressed after repeated exposure to the depressed states of their patients. Do they leave it at work - or does it follow them home?

## *How to Protect Yourself and Be Without Fear*

The best healers have been known to fall. I've seen even the most powerful masters overdue it and get depleted from seeing too many patients. Others seem to have no problems like this. So what is the key? I believe it is faith in God that is the key! I cannot tell a lie. That is what I believe. The TRUE SOURCE is the true source and there is no other true source. *For it is your personal relationship with the True Source that determines whether you are doing a "Qi Healing" or a "Miraculous Healing".* There have been a few great healers who can perform miraculous healing all the time. Jesus is a classic, the ultimate example. He said it best: "Your faith alone has healed you." Therefore, I always address the 'belief' of the recipient before sending any Qi. Also, I never charge money for sending God's blessing. Its ok to charge for a chiropractic adjustment, a massage or health evaluation—but "Qi Transmission" is truly God's work. I believe that removing the money compensation is one of the things that 100% protects the healer. Don't even accept a donation. I realize this is my philosophy and that not everyone agrees. We love all people & respect all beliefs. This is just my way. Practicing Qigong before & after the session also makes your Qi greatly increased and circulates positive energy through the body afterwards to stay healthy.

# Healing Others with Nine-Breath Method

Faith is always number one. If you get caught up in the fact you're doing the healing your patient won't be able to receive a miraculous healing. Because this technique is so powerful and because the receiver almost always claims a tremendous Qi feeling in their body it is easy to lose sight of The Source. For me personally, this has been the greatest source of all miracles from Qigong. It is a sacred gift. After you can create the ecstatic experience in yourself, you can do it for others. *It is a way to "Breathe for Someone Else".* You are in effect taking in the External or Universal Energy in the air through your warrior breaths. Then a precise Tumo exhale sends it pulsing out your hands into the person. The better your Tumo skills are, the better the result. Relax and think about being humble. During the warrior breaths think about receiving Qi from True Source and during 9th exhale visualize Qi going into the recipient's body. This profound exhale can last 1-2 minutes or longer.

## Jeff's Protocol for 9-Breath Healing Session

*\*Advanced 9-Breath Method "Guided Hands on Healing" Audio CD can be used during a healing session and either played out loud for both people or listened to on an iPod by the healer only.*

1) Massage the area you want to work on. If appropriate, use thumbs to knead muscles like dough.
2) Intend to channel healing energy directly from God. Breath deep and slow.
3) Ask for help. Internally say how grateful you are for God's blessing in this moment.

4) Turn your face away from the receiver so as not to breathe on them. Perform Nine–Breath Method and Tumo energy out from your palms into the area needing healing. Don't strain yourself. Even in the midst of doing the actual technique bring your attention to God. Remember that your breathing is simply a tool for drawing energy and is not the source of the energy itself. Think it's "God's Air" you are breathing.

5) Pound, Tap, and Massage in between sets, if appropriate. The pounding moves stuck Qi.

6) Repeat again as often as you like to do the Nine–Breath Method and breathe life into the area. Alternate with pounding and transmitting Qi in cycles. \*\*\* Don't be afraid of picking up bad Qi. Fear ruins the session. You are protected by God.

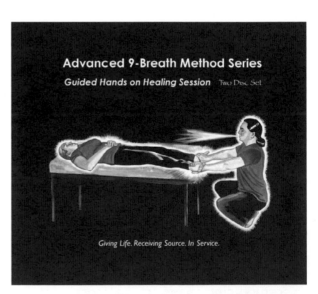

*If you enjoy giving Reiki and hands on healing, your energy will expand 10-fold using 9-Breath Method. Electric pulsating wave moves thru both the giver and receiver.*

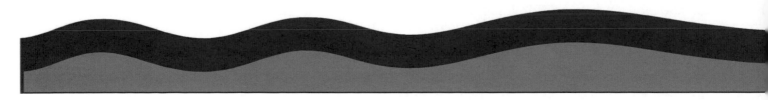

# Responses from Western Medicine

## *Qigong Experiences*

# Qigong Testimonials from Medical Doctors

Nurses and Medical Doctors are talking about Qigong, which we believe is poised to be the next major social wellness phenomenon. Each time we give the "Qigong Healing & Miracle Making" seminar we are overjoyed by the number of Nurses attending. Both nurses and medical doctors are looking for natural ways to take care of themselves. SSQC believes that Western Medicine serves a vital role in health care. We are excited and honored that so many within this field have come to us for training in Qigong movement exercise, advanced breathing exercise & Food-based Healing. Below are their written testimonials given after taking the 4 day Qigong seminar:

*"I have 30 Years Experience in Yoga, Tai Chi, and Qigong and I have never felt energy like this before. This system combines Qigong with Advanced Breathing Exercises that I've found PHENOMENALLY ENERGETIC. I'm now teaching this style of Qigong." - **Rick Agel M.D., Vascular Surgeon - Atlanta, GA**

*"This is definitely the most powerful workshop I have ever attended. The Qigong experiences were at a level that few things in life can compare to. In the workshop I could feel the love of 500 others!"*
*- **George Munoz M.D., Physician - Miami, FL***

*"Your Qigong Healing seminar was amazing! Very practical ways for everyone to harness the healing energy that is around us all. SSQC's food-based healing guidelines are practical & easy to implement. I'm absolutely certain about the amazing power of foods to heal & to keep us vibrant through our lives."*
*- **Alexander Doman M.D., Physician - Atlanta, GA***

*"The chronic tension I had in my neck & shoulders has really decreased a lot. The feeling of the energy was really strong from the very first exercise. Sometimes the Qi was so strong that it made me cry tears of Joy. This Qigong workshop has a well balanced combination of Qigong techniques & spirituality. Thank you for making it available to everyone."* *- **Marie Downer M.D., Microbiologist - Atlanta, GA***

*The Supreme Science Qigong Center's methods of collecting Qi are innovative, practical, & creative. They've taken the essence of various masters & condensed them, designing totally unique methods for our benefit. Their seminars are of immense value. Highly recommend for healthcare professionals."*
*- **George Dias M.D., Family Physician - Sydney Australia***

*"My injured knee now has no more pain! This was a great experience of Qi and felt great. Thank you for following your path to share this healing knowledge."* *- **Rocio Loor M.D. - W. Palm Beach, FL***

*"Your Qigong workshop is powerful, well taught, and emphasizes a scientific approach to healing."*
*- **Eve Hanna M.D., Occupational Medicine - Tampa, FL***

*"Jeff's workshop gives very powerful healing tools. I will be showing some of my patients!"*
*- **Joel Fernandez M.D., Physician- Tampa, FL***

# Qigong Testimonials from Nurses

*"Asthma has plagued me since childhood. Usually I need to use my Inhaler 5 times per day, but after the 1st days Breath Empowerment exercise we did on the floor...I only needed it 2 times. This is a definite improvement for me. The coaching of our breathing was really a true gift. This seminar is absolutely perfect!"- **Nancy Altman, Registered Nurse - Santa Fe, NM***

*"More energy than I have ever experienced before! It was so very powerful! Every part of me was vibrating. I particularly like the details on the Qigong they make sure you understand." - **Maggie Degenaro, Nurses Assistant***

*"After receiving a new mitral valve in 2002 climbing one flight of stairs exhausted me. After the 3rd day of the Qigong workshop I walked three flights of stairs to my hotel room and to my amazement I wasn't out of breath and my legs did not cramp as they usually do. From now on I'll use the stairs! Thank you for sharing your healing!" - **Joanne Saxion, Registered Nurse - Lakeland, FL***

*"This Qigong workshop enhanced my ability to feel energy and increase the intensity of it. Its given me a much better understanding as to why we do certain movements & breathing. Thank you for sharing. I love the message this work gives to humanity." - **Annie Yew, Registered Nurse - Orlando, FL***

*"I'm 70 years old and I have attended many seminars. This Qigong workshop was, without question, the BEST OF ALL OF THEM! I wish I had found it earlier in my life. Your Nine-breath Method Prayer circle is a profound experience." - **Lois Thompson, Registered Nurse & Counselor - Albuquerque,***

*"Very powerful concentrated experiences of Qigong & Energy in ALL activities. Also, very professional handling of 400 people keeping the energy alive & increasing for all 4 days of the Qigong workshop!" - **Denise E. Anderson, Registered Nurse - Albuquerque,***

*"Your Qigong demonstrations have profound healing potential. I will continue to practice the exercises. Great job containing the Qi of the room and having it flow smoothly. I loved the presentations in the evening, which reaffirmed my spiritual beliefs about "giving back to society". These presentations have contributed positively to ALL of our lives." - **Lily H. Bill, Registered Nurse - Albuquerque, NM***

*"I had a tightness for the past few months in my left shoulder blade. After all the Qigong practices on the 2nd day my friend gave me a tiny massage and it "totally broke up" and is gone completely now on this 4th day. I know that Qigong heals!" - **Rita Gugliotta, Registered Nurse - Santa Fe, NM***

*"This was my first experience with using the Qi-Energy in my life. Qigong has shown itself to be very worthwhile and I plan on practicing daily." - **Nita Chopra, Registered Nurse - Velarde, NM***

# Qigong Testimonials from Nurses *(Continued)*

*"The group energy was so profound. To experience the love, peace, joy, and healing for 4 days was life-changing. I loved your emphasis on correct Qigong form and making sure we got the important subtleties of Qigong. You will probably never know all the miracles you caused!"*
**- Deborah Marino, Registered Nurse, Palm Beach, FL**

*"It blows my mind the knowledge you and your instructors imparted! Your sincerity & passion for what you do is wonderful to see. This workshop has been a real joy." - **Marvel Myers, Licensed Practical Nurse - Tampa, FL***

*"The vibration, heat, and power we all felt during the Nine-Breath Method circle was profound. I felt a progressively stronger sense of Qi as the workshop went deeper. Lots of Joy, Peace, and Love."*
**- Linda Chapman, Licensed Practical Nurse - Sarasota, FL**

*"Absolutely life changing seminar! I felt peace and connected to 'The Source'. I plan to use what I learned in my daily life for the highest good." - **Patricia Dickenson, Registered Nurse - Ocala, FL***

*"I am already feeling much more healthy from doing this Qigong. During the workshop I felt many health problems improve both physically & emotionally." - **Lin Thomas, Registered Nurse - Sanford, FL***

*"The spiritual philosophy of peace, harmony, love and compassion resonates through the entire Qigong workshop. Our world is ready for this style of teaching."- **Marielle Skille, Registered Nurse - Belleair, FL***

*"Unlike any other group experience I have ever had. The content was richer than my imagination and Jeff is a supreme teacher. From the start he was communicating on all levels at once delivering the whole enchilada." - **Ella Bartholomew, Registered Nurse - Hollywood, FL***

*"I had pain in my shoulder when I came into the workshop. After the first Qigong Session, the energy was vibrating strong inside my body. 20 minutes later and the following days I had no pain at all! Nine-Breath Method is especially good." - **Marion Gerner, Rehabilitation Supervisor - Sarasota, FL***

*"These teachings are very clear with concise language & high quality AV learning tools. The Qigong I learned in this workshop will certainly add to my practice & personal life."*
**- Donna Henderson, Registered Nurse - Keystone Heights, FL**

# Qigong Testimonials from Nurses *(Continued)*

*"I've attended a myriad of spiritual workshops with heavy hitters like Ram Das and Larry Dossey and the fact this 4-Day workshop is only $70 is amazing. The Nine-Breath Method was truly an incredible experience. Pulsating energy accompanied by bliss! I was able to see Qi for the first time and felt Qi to a higher degree than I have ever before in my life."*
**- Susan Bowers, Registered Nurse - Lancaster, SC**

*"Never have I felt such vitality. At times I felt pure Joy! I really believe you can change your life over one weekend. I can't thank you enough!"*
**- Lydia Lorie, Registered Nurse, Delray Beach, FL**

*"I have studied energy healing for over 20 years and there are no words in the human language to describe my experience in your Qigong healing seminar. I came here to learn how to heal physically, but what I learned went far beyond & impacted me on a deep spiritual level. I am walking away from this seminar a charged spirit & truly empowered!"* **- Laura Muchmore, Registered Nurse - Tampa, FL**

*"Having done healing energy work for 35 yrs, I'm amazed how much more aware I am now of my Qi! The scope and depth of all the material you presented is awesome. My body feels lighter, younger, and my senses heightened. I am so grateful."* **- Joanne Driscoll, Nurse Practitioner - Sarasota, FL**

*"The workshop is spiritually uplifting and profoundly enlightening! I learned so much about how powerful my energy is. I brought my mom, dad, daughter, and niece and we all had a wonderful time. Thanks for a perfect workshop."* **- Renee Cosentino, Registered Nurse - Boyton Beach, FL**

*"The Nine-Breath Method circle allowed me to pray on a very deep level. I felt that my focus & energy were enhanced & that my prayer actually reached the person I was praying for. Your ability to speak about God without offending was also great."* **- Nanette Barber, Registered Nurse - Las Vegas, NV**

*"This was a great Qigong workshop! I feel it has improved my personal energy and that which I share. You make the material approachable and accessible."* **- Mary Bahl, Registered Nurse - Orlando, FL**

*"The intense spiritual energy was so powerful. I was amazed and delighted with the integrity of Jeff and his group. I feel blessed to have been a part of this wonderful Qigong healing event."*
**- Margie Farwell, Registered Nurse - Sarasota, FL**

# Testimonials from Veteran Qigong Students

*"I've dedicated over 20 years to the energy arts. No system has been as powerful as this one. What I appreciated most were the subtle things like thumb placement and subtle energy spiraling. Other Qigong systems leave out these subtleties. Because of the subtleties within this system I experienced Qi around me as a very dense field." - **Steve Williams, Aspiring Jedi Knight - Ft. Laud., FL**

*"I've done Five Element Taoist Medical Qigong, 8 Treasures Qigong and others. Having had the honor of being in your presence, I feel like I've been supercharged! I have such respect for your knowledge and teaching abilities.  - **Vito Demalteris L.M.T., - Greenacres, FL**

*"I have studied under 5 Qigong masters for more than 10 years time and practice daily.  Surprisingly, I learned more on the first day of this workshop than in all my previous studies combined!  This is the real deal." - **Shawn Nelson, U.S. Army Veteran & Qigong Instructor - Atlanta, GA**

*"The Supreme Science Qigong Center has an excellent Qigong program.  The balance of beneficial to health, spiritual, educational and entertaining is perfect.  A highly recommended experience."* - **Roger Millen Ph.D., Tai Chi Instructor for 30 Years - Tampa FL**

*"Having practiced Qigong for 14 years & studied in China, I can report that Supreme Science Qigong Center has a more effective training, on every level, in just 4 days than any other courses I've taken. Within 4 days my digestion improved 70%."* - **Joe Capuano,  Massage Therapist - Woodbridge, CT**

*"In 15 years of Qigong practice — this is the most efficient method of learning and teaching Qigong I've ever come across.  Supreme Science Qigong Center has a very effective system of teaching."* - **Jennifer Downey, Qigong Enthusiast & Acupuncture Physician – Gainesville, FL**

*"Despite the fact that I've learned 7 different styles of Qigong, my ability to detect and feel energy was never very strong.  Now, after the SSQC workshop, my ability to project and send energy has increased substantially.  The SSQC program pays attention to the very important subtle details."* - **Jeff McConnell, Acupuncture Physician – St. Petersburg, FL**

*"For over 50 years I have practiced energy medicine.  I have a Doctorate of Medical Qigong from China and I'm also a Quantum Touch Instructor with a Ph.D. in healing sciences.   Jeff's workshop brought everything together and showed me there is tremendous power in this system of Qigong. Thank You!"* - **Reverend Dr. Dennis Alexander, Full Time Healer – St. Petersburg, FL**

# Keynote Presentations

Natural Medicine

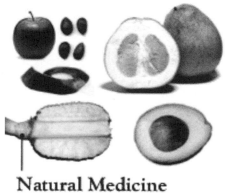

Art by: Jeff Primack

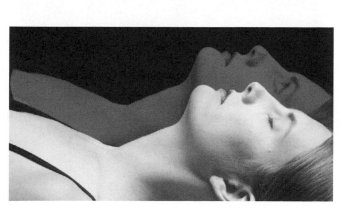

# Presentation #1
# Food Based Healing

Conquering ANY Disease... with the FOOD in your Grocery Store.

5-A-DAY.gov recommends 5-9 servings of fruits & vegetables.

They estimate very few people actually get it.

## Our Environment is 10 Times more toxic then it was only a decade ago.

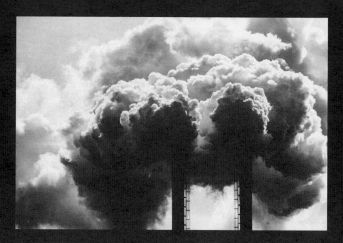

◆ We need to strengthen our immune system

◆ Nature has a provided the means to do this

# Phytochemicals
## ~Sparkplugs of the Immune System

◆ God has created a master healing device in each cell called the *Phase II Enzyme*. This process enables any cell to detoxify itself from chemical waste & toxins.

◆ The Phase II enzyme process is only possible when stimulated by phytochemicals. They act as spark plugs or "keys" that fit into cell receptors. They are the keys that start the rocket engine of your IMMUNE SYSTEM.

◆ Phytochemicals also carry a very high energy content and are the physical manifestation of the Lifeforce hidden inside the Tree-Yielding Seed and the tiny white hairs inside of a Strawberry flower!

# Where are Phytochemicals Located?

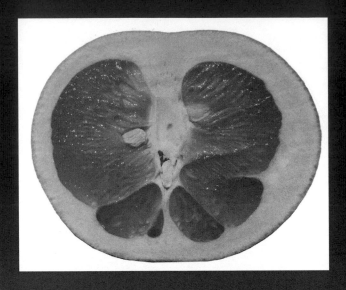

◆ The "bulk" of Phytochemicals reside in Cellulose Fibers. Juicing will be missing hundreds of special compounds that can only be found in the fiber.

◆ These are the white hairs on the strawberry and the crystals of the grapefruit. Its in the fiber... not the juice.

◆ Most people throw away the best parts of the food - the fiber - which is what contains God's healing medicine! We must use the whole food as God intended.

*But specifically where are phytochemicals found?*

# The Rind, Skin, Stems & Seed

*And God said, "Behold, I have given you every herb bearing seed, which is upon the face of all the Earth, and every tree, in which is a tree yielding seed; to you it shall be for meat." - Genesis Verse 1:29*

**God's Super-Potent Cancer Fighting Medicine**

# Your Body CAN Rejuvenate and Heal itself...
## *If given the Chance*

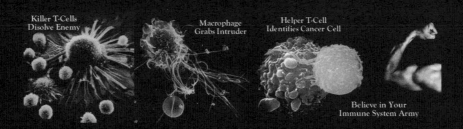

Killer T-Cells
Disolve Enemy

Macrophage
Grabs Intruder

Helper T-Cell
Identifies Cancer Cell

Believe in Your
Immune System Army

◆ The only permanent cure for disease is your body's own immune system. God has given you a powerful immune system army, *but it needs ammunition!*

◆ Your Immune System is strong enough to overcome ANY disease. In order to activate our immune system we need to give it a particular food that it LOVES. *Can we say it together? Phy-to-chem-icals!*

# 3-horsepower Blending Ideology

◆ If you chew an Apple with skin for a long time, most fibers still won't break. Look & see for yourself by spitting the chewed apple skin into a glass of water. The skin's fibers haven't even been broken yet!

◆ A 3 Horsepower Blender breaks the skins, seeds & stems into particle sizes that are beyond the micron level.

◆ We can then get the benefit of having chewed for several hours in a matter of minutes with this technology. A wise man said: "You are not what you eat, only what you absorb!"

*So Which Foods are Best For You?*

# We're about to tell you...

In a moment we'll be discussing ways that people have specifically reversed:

*Heart Disease

*Diabetes Type 1 & 2

*Cancer of ALL kinds

*Even great improvement for kids with Autism

*All from FOODS at the Grocery Store. But first...we need to know...*

# Are you excited?

Seriously... This is of monumental significance.

# Diabetes is Epidemic

## 30 Million Have it Now
## 60 Million Have Pre-Diabetes

*Mostly caused by Refined Foods and Lack of Phytochemicals in the Diet*

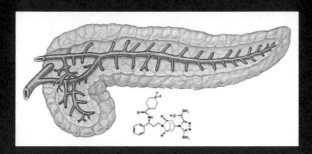

America Spends over $145 Billion on Diabetes Each Year.
*Two vegetables can change all that...*

# Swiss Chard

### Thousands of people have used this
### vegetable to naturally control blood sugar

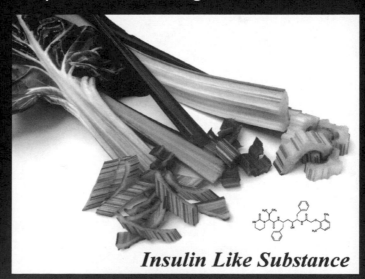

*Insulin Like Substance*

# Bitter Melon

## This one has the most "Insulin-Like Phytochemicals" of all vegetables

Both Type 1 & 2 Diabetics have balanced their blood sugar naturally be eating these and other special vegetables. However, this was in conjunction to following more food healing guidelines and eliminating may foods.

# Heart Disease

### America's #1 Killer... Every Minute an American dies of a Heart Attack

### 66% of Diabetics die of Heart Disease
### This Disease effects every person or someone they love

*People have naturally reversed "irreversible" arteriosclerosis with food & inexpensive mushrooms!!*

# Food Healing Strategy #1

## Remove Plaque from the Arteries

These foods have very high amounts of
"Soluble Fiber" to cleanse plaque out of the Arteries

# Food Healing Strategy #2

## Dilate Blood Vessels

 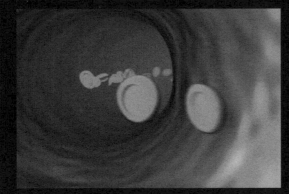 

Reishi Mushrooms are well documented in Japan to relieve Angina Chest Pain
Other varieties found at many grocery stores are cooked into stews and steamed.

# Food Healing Strategy #3
# Lower Blood Pressure if its High

It is a known fact in Chinese Medicine...
Eat 4-6 stalks of celery per day and blood pressure comes down

# Food Healing Strategy #4
# Lower Bad Cholesterol if its High

You can buy a bag of mushrooms for $3 at any
Oriental grocery store that naturally lowers bad cholesterol

# Cancer Epidemic
## Each year 1/2 million Americans do not recover

Our environment is becoming increasingly toxic causing immune system malfunction.
*AND* the lack of phytochemicals in most diets compounds the problem by keeping our immunity low.

*Thousands of people worldwide have **REVERSED** the "worst types"*
*of Cancer using a 3 Horse Power Blender & Readily Available Foods.*

# Beet: The Miracle Healer
## ~And the woman who reversed Pancreatic Cancer

*While this is extreme, we know that beet is one of the most important*
*foods for everyone, especially people with Cancer or Heart Disease.*

◆ In 2006, a Naturopathic Physician shared an amazing healing story with Jeff that really opened our eyes to the POWER OF BEET.

◆ A lady came to him with Pancreatic Cancer, because she had heard that others with this same type of cancer had successfully ***Reversed*** it following food-healing principles.

◆ The story ends with her shrinking a cancer the size of a watermelon in one month after consuming 6 pounds of beet everyday in a 3 Horsepower Blender!!

# Pineapple to Fight Cancer
## ~You've been throwing away the best part!

◆ Pineapple's reproductive energy is all in the stem. That's how you grow a new pineapple plant.

◆ Scientists in Queensland, Australia released research that there are many Anti-Cancer compounds in Pineapple stem.

◆ The effects mainly come from an increased response by our immune system. This is a natural immune system potenizing food!

# Many Foods Fight Cancer
## If you know what parts of the food have the medicine...

Our Program has detailed food guidelines that have been time tested effective for helping people's immune system heal itself...

## And that's the whole point...
# YOUR BODY KNOWS HOW TO HEAL ITSELF

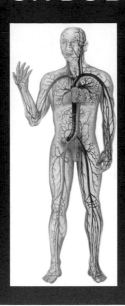

◆ No Food, Herb or Medicine can "Heal" you.
The Body Heals Itself... If given the fuel it needs.

◆ We were built to last longer than we are.
Man (and woman) used to be closer to nature.
It is time to INTEGRATE God's natural Medicine

### Genesis 6:3

*And God said, "My spirit shall not always strive with man, for he is also flesh: yet his days shall be a hundred & twenty years."*

## We're almost finished...
# One More Disease Needs to be Talked About

More children will be diagnosed with this disease in 2008 than with AIDS, diabetes and cancer combined.

# Exponential Growth

US Department of Education data from 1992 to 2001
indicates an average increase of 644% among all US children.

Autism is the fastest-growing
developmental disability.
10 - 17 % annual growth.

Current Estimates predict the rise in AUTISM
will surpass our ability to care for these children

# Autism Research Institute

◆ The **Autism Research Institute** has
evaluated various treatments of Autism since
1967.  Over 23,000 parents have responded
to their questionnaires to evaluate 77 types
of bio-medical intervention for autism.

*Mercury detoxification received a far higher
effectiveness rating than any drug, supplement,
or special diet.  Mercury detoxification was
rated helpful by 73% of parents!*

## Where does the Mercury come From?
## What might explain its 600% growth in the last 10 years?

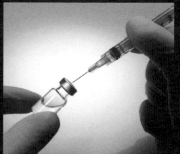

◆ Each year an estimated 40 tons of Mercury pollution moves through the air and into the sea from Coal-Burning power plants.

◆ New vaccinations of the last 20 years often use preservatives containing mercury

## Why does the Autism Research Institute correlate Mercury Toxicity to the Disease?

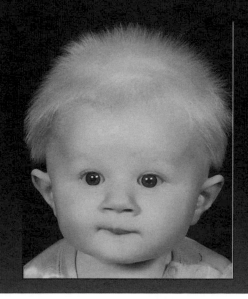

◆ It is a known that humans excrete heavy metals via their hair.

◆ Testing shows that babies with Autism have only 1/8th the amount of Mercury in their hair as normal babies do.
*Perhaps their ability to excrete Heavy metals is impaired?*

◆ Autistic baby's teeth on average have 300% more mercury than normal baby teeth

# Heavy Metal Toxicity is also strongly correlated with Alzheimer's & Fibromyalgia

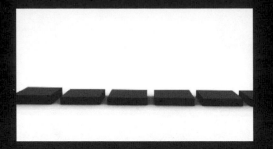

All of these diseases have been on the rise...
*So what can we do about all this Mercury in our environment?*

# We could live inside of bubbles...

# We have a better idea...

**CILANTRO**

**God's solution to
heavy metal toxicity**

Cilantro mobilizes heavy metals to come out of the spinal cord and brain.

# Parents Notice Dramatic Improvement...
# on Smoothies and the High-Phytochemical Diet

I'm a mother of twin boys with Autism. After learning the Dietary principles & Smoothie concepts at Jeff's Qigong Workshop my family has been blessed with the healthiest fast food ever. My Autistic twins were picky eaters and I have tried different supplements to improve their appetite, but they didn't work. They used to have low muscle tone, little coordination in there movements and had bathroom accidents even if they go to the potty beforehand. After 3 months preparing smoothies 1-2 times a day, their appetite improved dramatically. They began having different smoothies from the "Smoothie Formulas" recipe book, especially Cilantro. Soon they began to do things more independently, keep more instructions and understanding. Their muscle tone and awareness began to improve. They began to be more interactive and inviting to play more. The smoothies are a life saver for children and parents dealing w/Autism. My family enjoys the program very much!!!" - *Lynda Soto, Mother of Autistic Twins*

◆ 50% of kids with Autism are either constipated or have diarrhea

◆ They often won't eat "Ensure" and other synthesized foods.

◆ Kids with Autism are gulping down their smoothies. We add fruit and other high-phytochemical vegetables

# Food-Based Chelation of Heavy Metals and Big Huge Bowel Movements

◆ 90% of Mercury is eliminated through the stool.

◆ We all need BIG huge bowel movements.

◆ The "micronized" whole food high-phytochemical smoothie might be the most significant advancement in the healthcare.

# But how does it taste... Is it yukky?

◆ 15,000 people saw this presentation in live seminars from 2006-2009

◆ 90% were surprised by how good it actually tasted when they sampled it the first time.

◆ We have kitchen crafted recipes that WORK. Even people who never thought they could do something like this... are doing it.

# But do you Live on Smoothie?

## No... we don't live on Smoothie

Depending on whether or not you're a vegetarian or have a disease the protocol will be different.

*But there is something else you need to know...*

# Barbeque, Grilled Foods & Cancer
## ~3 Things you don't want!

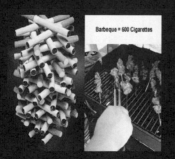 

No food or dinning experience is worth ending up in the hospital

◆ *Lancet British Journal of Medicine reports: 1 piece of BBQ NY Steak had the same carcinogen count as continuously smoking 600 Cigarettes!*

◆ *"Fire or Hot Metal" Directly Against Food chars the surface creating an abundance of carcinogens. Cook everything in a pot or pan with water or sauce!*

# Things Most People Don't Know

 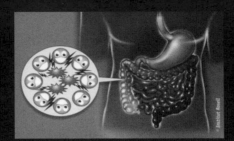

- Silica is more important for bone density than calcium.

- Probiotics (good bacteria) have been created in laboratories that can solve most digestive problems like IBS and Constipation

# Take Charge of Your Own Health

Don't rely on someone else to keep you healthy...
Its up to you.

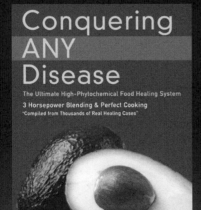

There are time-proven Specific  Food-Based protocols to help your body fight:

| | | |
|---|---|---|
| *Allergies | *Colds & Flu Virus | *Liver Diseases |
| *Alzheimer's | *Constipation & Digestive | *Menopause |
| *Arthritis | *Depression | *Migraines |
| *Asthma | *Diabetes Type 1 & 2 | *Osteoporosis |
| * ADD | *Eye Diseases & Poor Vision | *Parkinson's |
| *Autism | *Heart Disease & Stroke | *Prostate Disorders |
| *Poor Circulation | *Infertility | *Sexual Problems |
| *Cancer & Tumor | *Insomnia | *Thyroid Problems |
| *Chronic Fatigue | *Kidney Stones | *Weight Loss |

## Presentation #2

## Origin of the Universe, Miracles & Techniques for Manifesting Abundance

◆ Before the Big Bang…
The Taoists called it *The Void or Wuji*
The Kabbalists called it the *Endless World*
Its the oneness from which we all came!

◆ Why are we here?
*Difficult Question…simple answer*

◆ The Real Secret of Miracles
*That "The Secret" doesn't tell you about!*

# Miracles & Mind Attention

Miracles defy scientific rational thinking - yet they do happen.
They are a result of knowing that we exist within the Infinite Living Mind

# God said, "Let there be Light"

## And so it was...

Did the <u>True Source</u> need to "Do" anything to create the Light?

Or was the light created simply by God's Thoughts?

# We Live Inside...
# The Infinite Living Mind

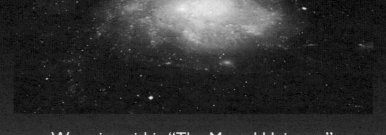

We exist within "The Mental Universe"
Created by the <u>thoughts</u> of the Original Intelligence

# What is the Universe MADE of?

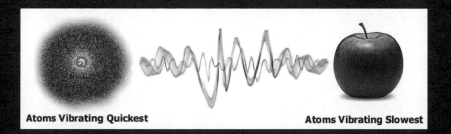

**Atoms Vibrating Quickest**    **Atoms Vibrating Slowest**

◆ Science already knows the truth about Solid Matter
Atoms consists of 99.99% empty space and are "Vibrating".

◆ From *Pure Spirit*, down to the condensed and slowed
down energy of an *Apple* - *all of creation is vibration*.

## "The True Source is Beyond Vibration"

## "The Original Intelligence is beyond form"

Our mind cannot comprehend
the totality of the True Source...

So what can be observed
about the Original Intelligence?

## Clearly Source Desires a Relationship with its creation
### *How do we know this?*

Through <u>Miracles</u> we can see the True Source has an "active" role in our evolution and plays a significant helping hand. It is through a trusting relationship with TRUE SOURCE that MIRACLES occur.

# So... What is a Miracle?

Life itself is a Miracle! The Sunrise is a Miracle!
There are countless miracles happening everyday!

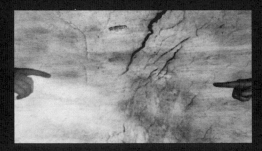

While this all sounds great... it is not how we use *the word* Miracle.

A True Miracle is undeniable. It shows that "*The Miraculous Event*" was so <u>statistically unlikely</u> that only an act of the INFINITE LIVING MIND could have brought its manifestation about.

# The First Creation...
# Individual Beings of Consciousness

**We are
Pure Spirit**

Our "Original Body" that was fashioned by the CREATOR is Pure Spirit
This Body of Energy is "Pure Consciousness" and is still our true nature even in this moment.

The Eye in the Pyramid came from the Masons who founded the USA.
It symbolizes our true nature which is PURE CONSCIOUSNESS.

# The Question of the Hour...
# "Why did God Create the Souls?"

God creates the Souls to experience the <u>sharing</u> of love. *God's nature is sharing.*
In order for God to share...there must be those who are "Desiring to Receive".
God imbues Souls with Desire to Receive. *Our nature is to enjoy receiving.*

# The Realm of Oneness

## ~According to the ancient Greek, Hebrew, and Yogic Sages

◆ In the beginning of creation, all the souls existed in the highest possible vibration of PURE SPIRIT. We were totally nourished and one with each other.

◆ The Location we began our existence was called:
"The Void" by the Yogic Masters
"Wuji" by the Qigong Masters
"Endless World" by the Kabbalists
"Our Father in Heaven" by the Bible

We were ONE WITH THE TRUE SOURCE and received GOD'S spiritual light indefinitely.
*We were totally fulfilled in a perfect existence.*

# Why then did we lower our vibration from the perfection of pure spirit?

*There was a longing that developed…*
*One which could not be fulfilled in The Realm of Oneness*

*After eons of time receiving God's light indefinitely…*
*We desired to have the experience of SHARING.*
*To be like the creator.*

*It was the first desire we had that couldn't be fulfilled.*
*Everyone was receiving the infinite light of True Source*
*and thus there was no Soul that lacked anything.*
*(No one to share with)*

**This presented a desire that could not be met in the Highest Heavenly Realm.**

# Endless receiving Gives us no more enjoyment...

◆ The Soul's desire to Share could not be fulfilled in the Endless World.  <u>We asked</u> God for an opportunity to experience sharing.

**<u>The Infinite Living Mind said something like this</u>:**

"Yes, I realize you want to share, but in order to do that I must create an environment where lack is possible. Darkness is the only way for you to share the light."

# Sure... We Can Handle It

Instantaneous Big Bang Occurs.  For the first time there is Duality. Yin & Yang.  Male / Female.  Multi-Dimensional Universe is created.

*The opportunity for sharing occurs now, because there is possible Having/Not Having.*

# Earning the Light

We asked TRUE SOURCE to set it up so that we could have
the experience of earning the light/blessing through our actions.

System of Karma was created so we can <u>Earn</u> the Light.
Instead of being given everything…we asked to earn it instead.

## This Helps explain the age old question:

# Why Are We Here?

All of us had the same Goal.
To be like our Father (Creator).

To transform from a being of
Receiving into a being of Sharing.

***We wanted to EARN God's
Blessing instead of receiving it
endlessly in the Realm of Perfection

*This is "Why we are here". (In the realm of Light & Dark)… And this is why it feels "Right" to Help.*
*Notice children get really excited at the prospect of actually helping you. Children instinctually know this secret.*

# The Reality

- We are receiving everything from the True Source.
- One cannot share without receiving.
- The Miracle Making Secret:   Receiving for the sake of sharing

***This is fulfilling our original purpose for coming here.

# Receiving Alone doesn't Work

Have you ever had someone do everything for you?
We resent people the most who help us <u>without us earning it</u>.

*Playing Hard-to-Get Works because it makes the person feel they are "Earning" and thus they will be happy.*

# True Happiness

*Happiness comes from sharing... therefore we must learn to receive for the sake of sharing*

\*\*\* When we share beyond our comfort zone a great amount of light is revealed.
This is a powerful technique to develop spiritually - - Its called TRUE SHARING.

*During a moment of True Sharing our <u>original nature</u> will arise and attempt to get us to think of ourselves.*

# The Opponent

There is an invisible enemy.  It is the ego.
Also known as the desire to receive for ones self alone.

*It was originally called "SET" by the Egyptians.*
*Later it became known as the SETAN force of Christianity.*

# Acknowledging the Enemy

◆ The Set (Satan) is a very real force inside us all.

◆ Perhaps the most misunderstood of all religious concepts.

◆ It seeks to 'Trick' you into thinking of yourself alone.

◆ To deny the existence of the enemy makes it stronger.

# How it Works

**My Anger is Your Fault**

**I know that I'm Right**

**Getting the Last Word**

## These are all forms of TAKING Receiving for the Self Alone

# Resist the Ego (Miracle Blocker)

In order to practice a HIGHER LEVEL OF QIGONG we resist the desire to receive for one's self alone.

This is a REAL BATTLE. The ego (satan) does not quit - even after we become "spiritual".

*The ego is weakened by True Sharing. What is True Sharing? What does it mean to resist?*

# Doing a good deed… and not telling <u>anyone</u> about it.

***The Real Story of Santa***

The father planned to stay awake to find out who was helping his daughters. He dozed off, but heard a small "clink" as another bag landed in the room. Quickly he jumped up and ran out the door. Who did he catch ducking around the corner?

Nicholas, the young man who lived with his uncle. "Nicholas, it is you! Thank you for helping us—I hardly know what to say!" Nicholas said, "Please, do not thank me—thank God that your prayers have been answered. Do not tell others about me."

Listening to someone else's view even though it opposes yours...

Listening without thinking about what you're going to say...

These are powerful forms of SHARING

# This moment is actually an opportunity

◆ Can we hear opposing views and simply listen?

◆ This is actually a TECHNIQUE for manifesting Higher Levels of Qigong. Its called, "Cultivation"

# Taoist Cultivation *is not only about Qi*

◆ Ancient Qigong Masters knew about the power of Miracles.

◆ They knew that mediation alone was not enough to reach the goal.

◆ Taoists masters, like Peng Tzu pictured left, practiced an invisible form of "cultivation" that attracted the blessing from the SOURCE.

# Sharing is Easy
# True Sharing by definition is not...

# The Harder it is to NOT REACT...
# The more LIGHT IS REVEALED if we are successful

*You will hear the Ego's Protest and discomfort during a moment of true sharing. That is when we resist the desire to <u>react</u> to that voice.*

# Pause and see the bigger picture

Instead of saying something that glorifies yourself... Resist!
Instead of instantly reacting to someone's wrong words... Resist!
Instead of taking credit for good deeds... Be like Saint Nicolas!!!
***Resist the self-focused voice. Go against the desire to receive for the self alone.*

# Padre Pio

## *Someone who clearly understands the miraculous*

During World War 2 pilots from allied forces were bombing areas of Italy.
They tried to bomb San Giovanni, Padre Pio's home town, on many occasions.
Each time the squadrons would see this "Friar" appear in the sky with arms held out.

Allied forces believed there were weapons stored in this town.
Finally the head commander flies over to do the job himself. He sees the same Friar in the sky.
Not a single bomb ever fell in San Giovanni. This commander later met Padre Pio in the town. He bowed to him.

# Humble is the Way

## Jesus washed the feet of his disciples to show he was humble.

When we realize God's Blessing is "what matters most" then we understand how small & futile our human efforts
are without the blessing from the Supreme. Being humble is a way of asking for support from True Source.

*\*It is the key of all great teachers*

# Prosperity Benefits of True Sharing

When you give of yourself beyond your comfort zone… you will obtain *true prosperity*.
It is the fastest way to grow financially. If you need money… Be willing to share money!
If you need time… Be willing to share time!

# Health Benefits of True Sharing

You'll SAVE energy for your body to heal!
Negative emotions are the #1 cause of disease

# The missing piece of the puzzle
## *God's Blessing*

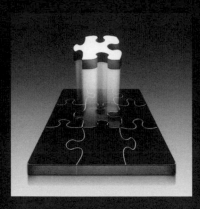

◆ The Blessing from Source is the single most powerful force in the universe.

◆ It is our belief: That in order for the teachings of Law of Attraction or "The Secret" to work that prayers must be POTENIZED by thinking of others and a practice known as TRUE SHARING.

◆ Remember - We <u>asked</u> the Creator to Earn the Blessing so that we would be fulfilled on our deepest level.

Disclaimer: We do not claim to know the absolute truth.
It is our understanding that Manifestation of Miracles and Prosperity are only possible through sharing.

# Presentation #3
# The Afterlife - A Scientific Perspective

◆ 1000's of documented cases show when people die they "float up" out of their body and can see events taking place around them.

◆ Sam Parnia M.D. writes accounts shared from dozens of surgeons on reports of people who've died on the operating table from cardiac arrest.

◆ Many bring back knowledge of the Life Contract. *Yes, we all signed it.*

*In today's hospitals people are being "revived" after being clinically dead for 90 minutes.*

# Culturally Universal Experience

◆ Floating out of the body and being witnesses to surrounding events
◆ Entering a long tunnel or door with light at the end
◆ Seeing a world of unimaginable beauty and deceased loved ones
◆ Being told they "must go back" because they have something to do

# Case #1: The Missing Teeth

In this standard "cardiac arrest" the Nurse reports removing a patient's dentures and placing them in a drawer of special trolley after the attempt to restart the heart had gone on for 90 minutes. He survived, but lost his teeth.

1 week later the man returned to where the Nurse had worked. He saw her and said, "Yes, you were there when I was brought into the hospital and you took the dentures out of my mouth and put them into that cart. It had all these bottles on it and there was a sliding drawer underneath and that's where you put my teeth."

When the nurse questioned him further it appeared the man had seen himself lying in bed and had perceived from above how the nurses and doctors were busy with CPR. He was also able to describe in exact detail the room in which he had been resuscitated as well as the appearance of those present.

# The relationship between the Mind & Brain

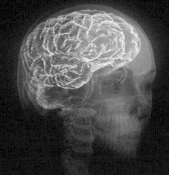

Medical science still believes consciousness is produced by the brain *(Ha Ha!)*

*How could thought processes, memory formation, and reasoning be "heightened" at a time when there is no brain function for hours? - - - Science demonstrates that our mind-consciousness is **not** produced by the brain.*

# How our Brain is like a Television

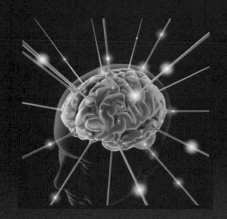

When we look at the sub-atomic level... solid matter exists in the form of electrons, quarks and further light & sound waves. Not just our physical body, but our thoughts & consciousness. *Consciousness is itself a subtle type of matter similar to electromagnetic waves (like the ones your cell phone interprets).*

Modern medical science currently does not understand **how** consciousness is produced. They still believe consciousness is sourced from the Brain, which is sort of like a small child watching Television. If a child doesn't understand how a TV works, they may believe the presenter is actually *sitting in* the TV!

The child can test his theory by pulling a few wires out of the television set, and sure enough, there will be a loss of sound & picture...thus confirming that all that is being seen and heard *is coming from inside the TV.*

*It is also possible that the TV set (our brain) is simply acting as a receiver.*
*Yes, we need the TV to perceive thoughts, but its actually a <u>RECEIVER</u> (not the source of thought).*
*The actual source of thought is the "Mental Body or Spirit Body" that survives death.*

# Case Example: 2 Year Olds NDE

His mother tells the story: "John's heart had stopped. The doctors were pressing on his chest and he was lifeless and blue. They brought him to the hospital in an ambulance."

After he had been discharged from the hospital one day during the course of play he said, *"When I died, I saw a lady."* I asked the family if anyone had mentioned anything to him about dying. Nobody had... John said, *"When I was in the doctor's car, the belt came undone, and I was looking down from above."* He also said, *"When you die, it's not the end... a lady came to take me...there were many others who were getting new clothes, but not me, because I wasn't really dead. I was going to come back."*

Interestingly, John's parents noticed that he kept on drawing the same picture over and over again. As he got older, it got more complex. When asked what the balloon was, he said *"When you die you see a bright lamp and...are connected by a cord."*

# John's Drawing

# Case Example:  3 Year Olds NDE

Andrew's mother tells the story: "At 3 years old he was admitted to the hospital with a heart problem and had to undergo open heart surgery."

"Two weeks after the surgery Andrew started asking *when he could go back to the beautiful sunny place with all the flowers & animals.*

I said, "We'll go to the park in a few days when you're feeling better". "No," he said, "I don't mean the park, I mean the sunny place I went to with the lady." I asked, "What lady?" and he said, *"You didn't take me there. The lady came and got me. She held my hand and we floated up…you were outside when I was having my heart mended…it was okay. The lady looked after me; the lady loves me. It wasn't scary; it was lovely. Everything was bright and colorful, but I wanted to come back to see you."*

# Elizabeth Taylor

<u>In an interview with America's AIDS magazine, Liz described her NDE</u>:

"I went to that tunnel, saw the white light, and Mike (Elizabeth Taylor's 3rd Husband who died in a plane crash). I said, Oh Mike, you're where I want to be. And he said, 'No, Baby. You have to turn around and go back because *there is something very important for you to do. You can't give up now.'* It was Mike's strength that brought me back."

# Donald Sutherland

Donald Sutherland had a near-death experience when ill with meningitis in 1979.

*"Suddenly the pain, fever and acute distress seemed to evaporate. I was floating above my body, surrounded by soft blue light. I began to glide down a long tunnel, away from the bed ... but suddenly I found myself back in my body. The doctors told me later that I had actually died for a time."*

# Gary Busey

In 1988, Gary was going about 40-50 miles per hour riding on 750 pounds of cold steel. He was not wearing a helmet when he crashed. He was flung over the top of his cycle, head first into the curb and he cracked his skull. Busey had a NDE while he was dying on the operating table after having brain surgery.

During his NDE, he was surrounded by angels. Busey stated that they didn't appear in the form that people see on Christmas cards. The angels he saw were big balls of light that floated and carried nothing but love and warmth - and this love is unconditional.

# Statistics on NDE

## THE GALLUP ORGANIZATION

The most respected poll in 1992 estimated that that 13 million Americans had experienced a NDE. The population of the United States in 1992 was approximately 260 million, leading to an estimate of NDE prevalence of 13 mil/260 mil, or 5%.

# Logical Conclusion

◆ Scientific Observation and Research worldwide has undoubtedly PROVEN that our consciousness travels to a beautiful place upon death.

◆ Many bring back knowledge of a Divine Plan or Life Contract and many return because specific parts of the contract have not been realized.

# Past Lives and the Hard Evidence

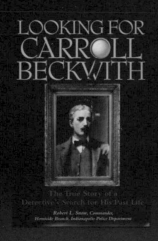

Robert Snow, Indianapolis homicide commander, was the biggest skeptic of them all. On a dare, he participated in (and taped) a "Past Life Regression" with a psychologist.

# Detective Investigation

◆ His experience in hypnosis was as vivid as watching a movie. He came away with 28 vivid details from a past life *(tape recorded)*.

◆ He saw a painting clear in his mind. Using his detective skills, he searched everywhere to find this painting so that he could prove that he had seen it somewhere, and that it not been a past-life image.

*The length to which Police Captain Snow goes to <u>prove himself wrong</u> and then has to accept the truth is amazing. Captain Snow does not readily accept any of the evidence, but validates it thoroughly with police like reliable research methods.*

# Putting the Pieces Together

Eventually, it was a synchronistic event which broke the case--while on vacation, exploring art galleries in New Orleans, he suddenly found himself face-to-face with the unusual portrait he had seen himself painting in the regression session.

After running into this obscure painting - he had the painter's name!!!
*James Carroll Beckwith*

# Positive Identification

◆ Upon learning the painting was James Carroll Beckwith's he conducted an extensive search on his life details.

◆ Through a miracle, he finds the house Beckwith lived in and obtains Beckwith's diary.

*Of the 28 specific memories that Snow had documented from the regression, such as the painting of the hunchback woman, the cause of his wife's death, logistics of his home and career - 26 were verified in the written diary.*

# Objective Evidence for Past Lives is Overwhelming

Verified correct by historians... information gleaned from regressions is often precisely accurate.

Co zescie zrobili?

People Often Speak Perfect in Languages They Never Learned

Phobias suddenly disappear after pastlife memories recall the cause.

Birthmark in same location as severe injury recalled from previous life

# Past Life Regression tells us something important about this life

In many cases the person begins talking about their lives before the present lifetime… *And about the time in-between lives including the <u>planning</u> of the present lifetime.*

# If past lives are a certainty...

1st Conclusion: You've lived many times under different conditions

# If past lives are a certainty...

2nd Conclusion: There is a reason you chose this body

# If past lives are a certainty...

3rd Conclusion: There is a reason you chose your parents

# If past lives are a certainty...

4th Conclusion: There is a reason you chose your birthplace

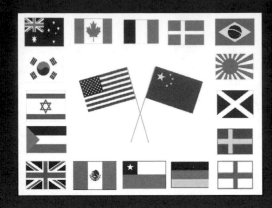

# If past lives are a certainty...

5th Conclusion: We prefer our REAL Home on the other side

Shamans & Tribal people talk of the "Other Side"
as being a place without war, sickness, and of great beauty.

*** *Why then, did we come here in the first place?*

# If past lives are a certainty...

### 6th Conclusion: There is a structured plan in place

*If we continue coming back, even though every soul wants to stay there...*
*We must be coming here for a reason. There must be a plan and an objective to our visit.*

# Life Contract

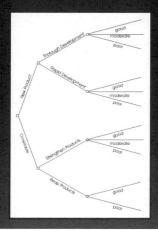

◆ Many ancient masters & scriptures have discussed the Life Contract.

◆ Very complex, the Life Contract forms a "Decision Tree" which means it contains many outcomes for different possible choices.

No matter how wonderful & blessed your life is...
No matter how painful & chaotic your life is...

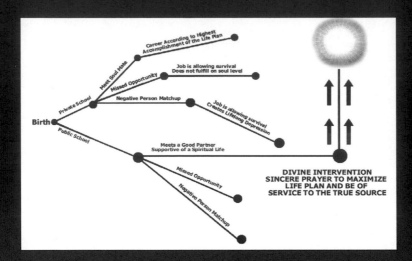

*The __sincere prayer__ to TRUE SOURCE declaring your firm commitment to maximize your Life Plan and be as useful as possible in SERVICE is the KEY!*

# The Magic Question

Are you following the Highest Possible Path stated in YOUR LIFE PLAN?

*What are the signs that you are headed in this direction?*

# Miracles that assist your current direction

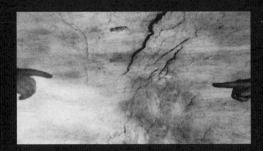

The Planning of your Life was a Long and Detailed Affair...
You asked for Miracles to Manifest when you are on the Right Path!

*These are miracles of an undeniable nature.*
*When they happen you will undoubtedly sense the Higher Power behind it.*
*Nothing is more powerful than this DIRECT INTERACTION with the True Source!*

---

# People that assist your current direction

*The Planning of your Life was a Long and Detailed Affair...*
*You asked for The Right People to Manifest when you are on the High Path!*

Following your purpose will in itself show many signs that the "Universal Intelligence" is bringing you all the RIGHT PEOPLE to support your contribution to society.

These PEOPLE are undeniably brought to you by the True Source. You will feel these people have a presence in your life of *profound importance*.

# A feeling of REAL PURPOSE from your Career

Following the highest path in your life plan will show many signs...
Including a Job that gives fulfillment on the deepest levels.

*This is a JOB undeniably brought to you by the True Source.*
*You will feel this job has profound importance in your life and the lives of others.*

# What are the signs that you might NOT be fulfilling your life plan?

*1) A lack of True Undeniable Miracles in your life.*

*2) Friends and partners who do not support you in living a spiritual life*

*3) A lack of real fulfillment in your life's work.*

# How do you know the best choice for something really important?

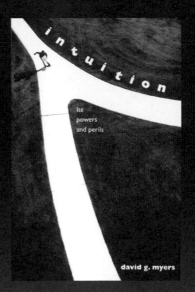

◆ New Age thought advocates using intuition for making important choices.

◆ Author David Myers says, "While intuition can provide us with useful and often amazing insights… it can also dangerously mislead us."

*We teach that intuition is useful, but not the best method of knowing the right choices. So what is better than our intuition that is not prone to error or emotional clouding?*

# A Direct Sign from God!

*If you ask the True Source for "signs" to lead you in the right direction, they will undoubtedly be given.*

One of the best meditations is to ask the True Source for a "Direct Sign"
*Something unmistakable that is so profound it cannot be coincidence*

# A Most Powerful Prayer

*"True Source, creator of all things, all beings, and all life everywhere. I see that you are the most capable advisor. Please show me a direct sign of a miraculous nature with regards to X situation.*

*I ask that you make the sign so far beyond coincidence so that I will have absolutely no doubt it came from you."*

# Presentation #4
## Sacred Geometry, History of the Universe & Humanity's Future

◆ Sacred Geometry appears everywhere in Nature, from the leafs on plants to the proportions of our bodies.

◆ The Stars, Galaxies and Galaxy Clusters show us the "Elastic Nature of Reality".

◆ Many architectural wonders of the world hint that human potential is *just beginning to unfold*.

◆ The Future of Mankind is up to us. We can navigate our future in the positive direction.

# What is sacred about Sacred Geometry?

◆ It is the "Universal Language " exhibited by all life forms.

◆ Why is it important?   Because it can be seen in flowers, snowflakes, snails, galaxies, DNA, crystals, facial structure, and everything in all creation.

*Awareness of Sacred Geometry brought brilliant scientists like Pythagorus, Plato and Newton to a more tangible relationship with the Creator.*

# The Divine Proportion

Φ

◆ Plato in his views on natural science and cosmology presented in his "Timaeus," considered *Phi* to be the most binding of all mathematical relationships and the key to the physics of the cosmos.

◆ Leonardo Da Vinci provided illustrations for a dissertation published in 1509 entitled the "Divine Proportion." This book contains drawings made by Leonardo Da Vinci displaying *phi ratio proportions of the human body* as well as the 5 Platonic solids discussed later.

*\*\*\*There is no other specific number that recurs throughout life on Earth with such regularity as does Phi.*

# Phi Ratios in the Body

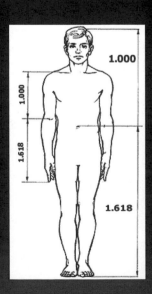

◆ Recall that Phi is a Ratio.
A Ratio compares the size of 2 different things.

◆ Regardless of who is being measured...
The distance from the "naval to the feet" is 1.618 times bigger than the distance from the naval to the top of the head!!!

◆ The length of the "elbow to the index finger" is 1.618 times greater than the length of the shoulder to the elbow!!!

*\*\*\*The Phi ratio appears in Facial Structure and countless body proportions.*

# Phi Ratio in our DNA

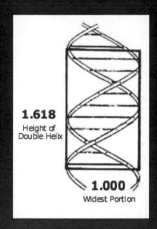

♦ The height of a double helix (two intersections) is 1.618 times greater than the width of the DNA!

♦ Phi is the Ratio found in all of creation.
*It could be said that Phi is the mark of the creator!!*

# Plant Growth

♦ If the central stem of a plant is looked at closely… As the plant grows upward, new branches grow off of the stem in a spiraling pattern.

♦ In an overwhelming number of plants, after a branch grows out of the stem, it grows some and then sends out another branch *137.5 degrees* relative to the direction of the previous branch. *Why is this significant?*

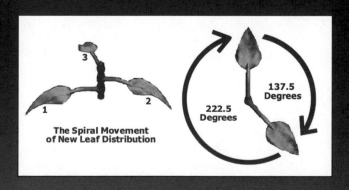

If you divide 137.5 degrees into the remaining portion 222.5 degrees you get that DIVINE NUMBER AGAIN!

222.5 / 137.5 = 1.618

# Phi is Ultra Efficient

◆ This exact amount of 137.5 Degree rotation causes the least amount of overlap. Not only beautiful, this means that each leaf receives the maximum amount of sunlight to assist in photosynthesis.

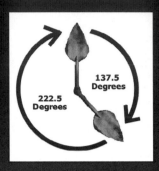

◆ The Phi rotation contributes greatly to the overall balance of the plant.

*The 137.5 degree rate of rotation governed by Phi is <u>the only number</u> that can produce such perfected efficiency (without overlapping leaves even after 10 offshoots).*

# Brief History of Phi

◆ The Divine Proportion was closely studied by the Greek sculptor, Phidias, and as a result, it took on the name of Phi.

◆ Greek sculptor Phidias was born 490 BC and sculpted many parts of the *Parthenon*.

◆ The exterior dimensions of the Parthenon form a perfect Golden Rectangle.

***During the Renaissance, renowned artists such as Michelangelo, Raphael, and Leonardo da Vinci also made use of Phi - for they knew of its appealing qualities.*

***1600 years after Phidias made use of Phi in Greek Architecture... its AMAZING significance was further seen by an Italian man who noticed patterns in flowers.*

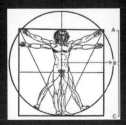

# The Fibonacci Sequence

♦ In 1175 AD Leonardo Fibonacci noticed a repeating pattern of number sequences in plant leaves.

*1, 2, 3 ,5 ,8, 13, 21, 34 etc...*

*The Fibonacci numbers are Nature's numbering system. They appear everywhere in Nature, from the flower petal arrangement in plants, to the bracts of a pinecone, and the scales of pineapple. The Fibonacci numbers are applicable to the growth of everything!*

# Fibonacci Examples

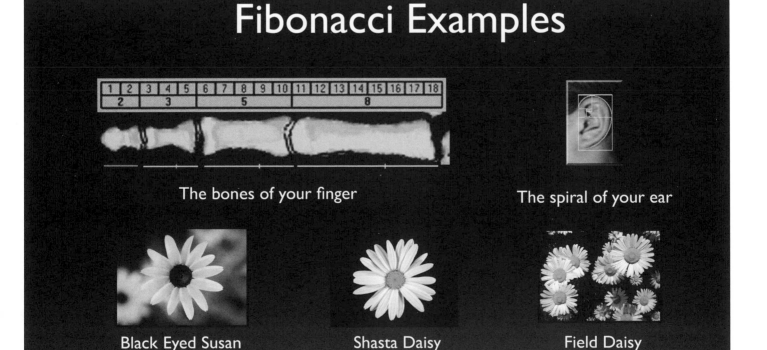

The bones of your finger

The spiral of your ear

Black Eyed Susan
13 Petals

Shasta Daisy
21 Petals

Field Daisy
34 Petals

## Fibonacci's Relationship to the Divine Proportion Phi

| Current Number | Previous Number | Division | Ratio |
|---|---|---|---|
| 1 | 1 | 1 // 1 | 1.0 |
| 2 | 1 | 2 // 1 | 2.0 |
| 3 | 2 | 3 // 2 | 1.5 |
| 5 | 3 | 5 // 3 | 1.6666 |
| 8 | 5 | 8 // 5 | 1.600 |
| 13 | 8 | 13 // 8 | 1.625 |
| 21 | 13 | 21 // 13 | 1.615384 |
| 34 | 21 | 34 // 21 | 1.619048 |
| 55 | 34 | 55 // 34 | 1.617647 |
| 89 | 55 | 89 // 55 | 1.618182 |
| 144 | 89 | 144 // 89 | 1.617978 |
| 233 | 144 | 233 // 144 | 1.618056 |
| 377 | 233 | 377 // 233 | 1.618025751 |
| 610 | 377 | 610 // 377 | 1.618037135 |

◆ As the Fibonacci numbers get larger… Their ratios against the previous number continue getting more and more aligned with the True Phi Ratio.

# Fibonacci Spiral

The F-spiral can be found in countless life forms on Earth and in Galaxies.

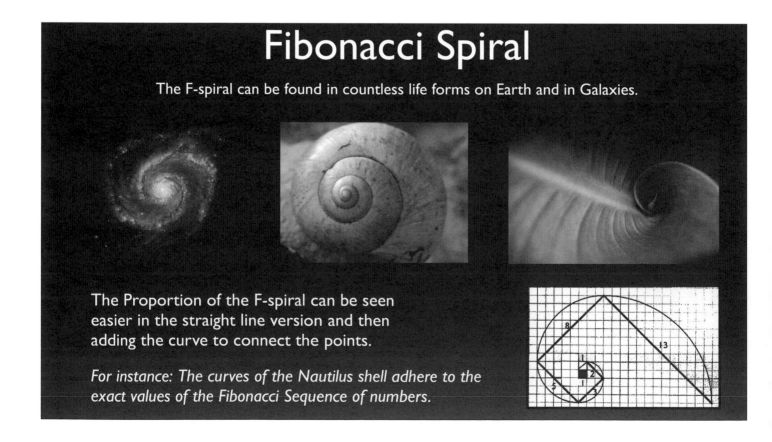

The Proportion of the F-spiral can be seen easier in the straight line version and then adding the curve to connect the points.

*For instance: The curves of the Nautilus shell adhere to the exact values of the Fibonacci Sequence of numbers.*

# Pyramid Arrangement

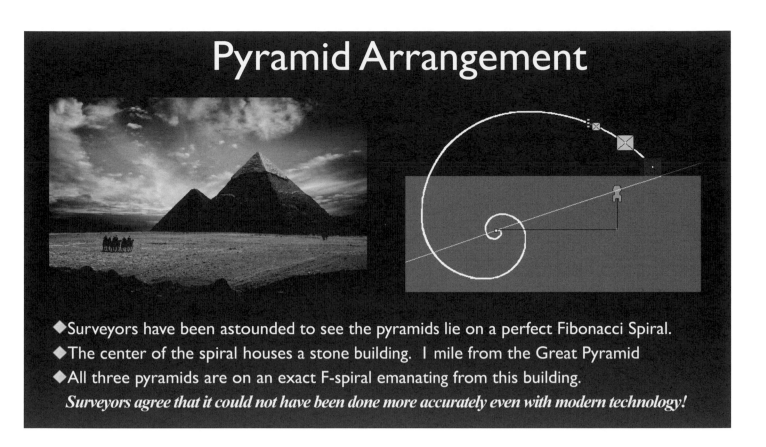

◆Surveyors have been astounded to see the pyramids lie on a perfect Fibonacci Spiral.

◆The center of the spiral houses a stone building.  I mile from the Great Pyramid

◆All three pyramids are on an exact F-spiral emanating from this building.

*Surveyors agree that it could not have been done more accurately even with modern technology!*

# Flower of Life

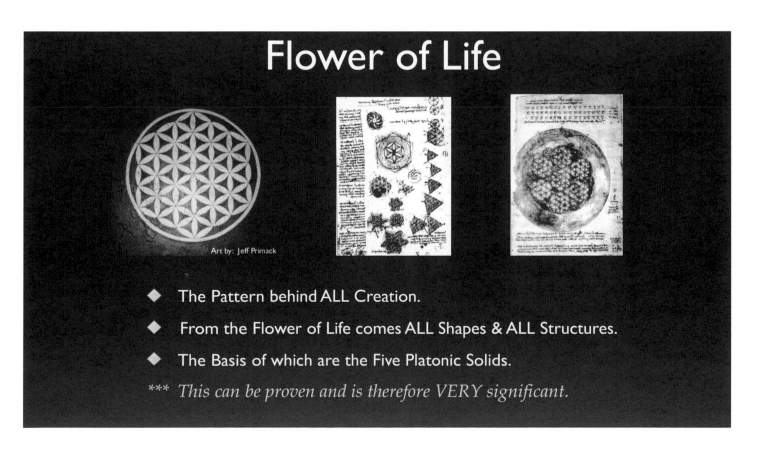

Art by: Jeff Primack

◆ The Pattern behind ALL Creation.

◆ From the Flower of Life comes ALL Shapes & ALL Structures.

◆ The Basis of which are the Five Platonic Solids.

*** *This can be proven and is therefore VERY significant.*

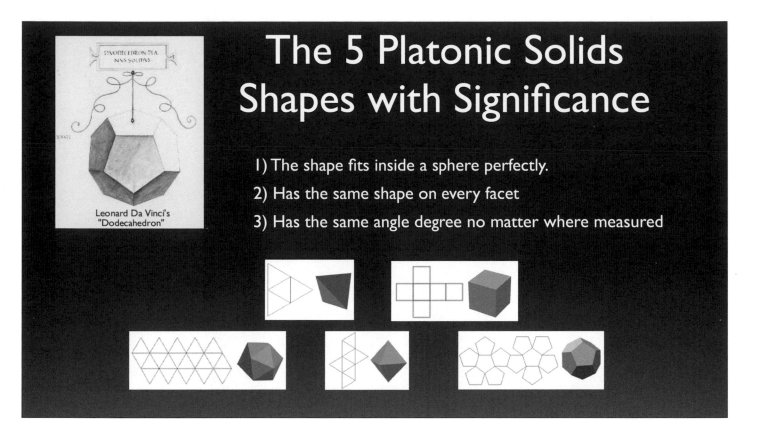

# The 5 Platonic Solids
# Shapes with Significance

Leonard Da Vinci's
"Dodecahedron"

1) The shape fits inside a sphere perfectly.

2) Has the same shape on every facet

3) Has the same angle degree no matter where measured

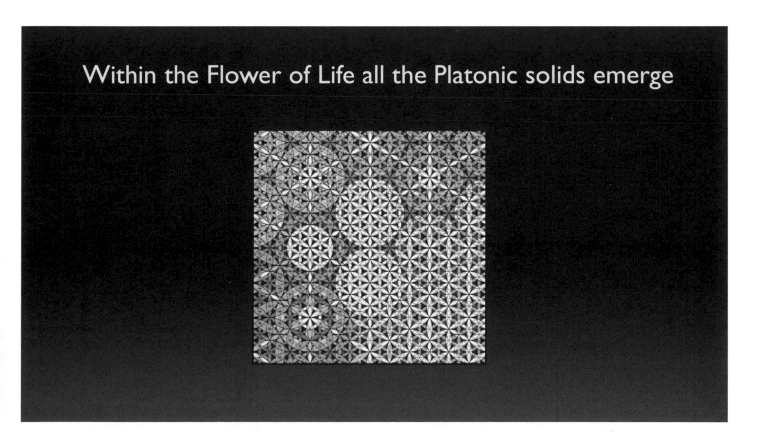

# Within the Flower of Life all the Platonic solids emerge

# Begin Drawing the Flower of Life

1) Draw a circle

2) Pick anywhere on the <u>edge</u> of your circle to place the needle of the compass.

3) Draw another circle.

# Vesica Pisces

- ◆ Union of Yin & Yang
- ◆ Basis for all creation
- ◆ Forms the Jesus Fish

*Continue drawing circles by placing the needle of the compass at <u>intersection</u> points.*

# You'll start to see a pattern
~It always makes SIX petals no matter where you begin from

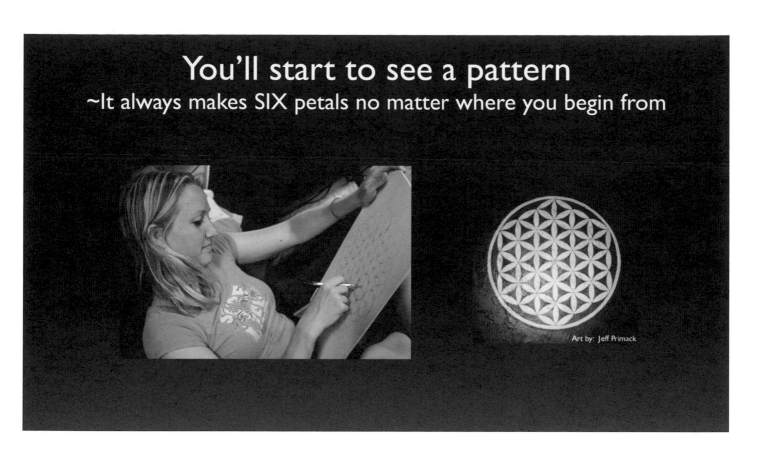

In order to see how the platonic solids form out of the Flower of Life...

## We must draw it out further. *This reveals "Fruit of Life"*

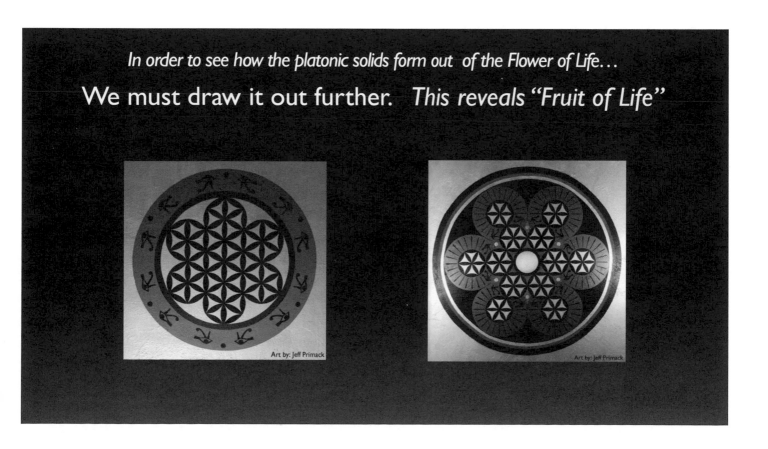

# Flower of Life Reveals
# Metatron's Cube

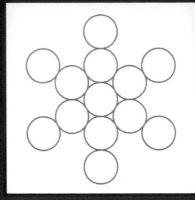

The secrets of the Flower of Life can only be seen by drawing the Fruit of life.

By connecting every center…
With every other center…
Metatron's Cube is Revealed.

# The 5 Platonic Solids...
# Hidden within Metatron's Cube

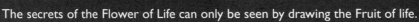

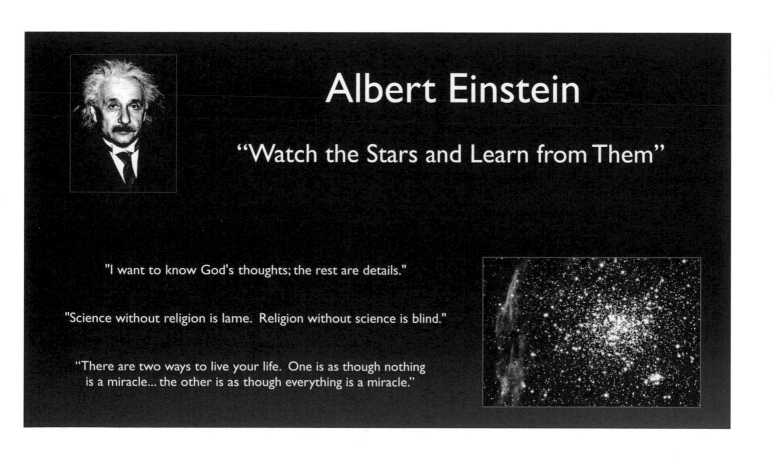

# What is a Star?

- A Star is a Nuclear Reactor.

- "Merging" Hydrogen Atoms together creates Helium & RELEASES ENERGY.

- At the Core of every star this process is occurring generating light and heat.

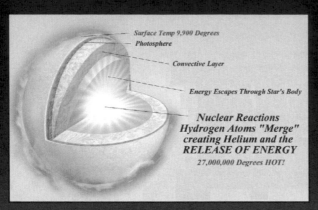

Surface Temp 9,900 Degrees
Photosphere
Convective Layer
Energy Escapes Through Star's Body

*Nuclear Reactions*
*Hydrogen Atoms "Merge"*
*creating Helium and the*
*RELEASE OF ENERGY*
*27,000,000 Degrees HOT!*

Helium

# The Sun's Massive Size

## Over 1,000,000 times the size of Earth

- Light is the *Positive* Energy of the Universe

- Gravity is the *Negative* Energy of the Universe

*The Yin/Yang balance between the Radiating Light, which would normally blast apart our sun, and the tremendous gravitational force from its density is what keeps our Sun held together.*

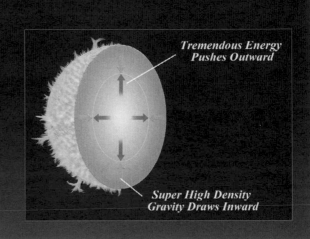

*Tremendous Energy*
*Pushes Outward*

*Super High Density*
*Gravity Draws Inward*

# The Fabric of Reality

In 2004 NASA & Stanford University launched a satellite (costing $750 million) to prove once and for all Einstein's Theory: That Gravity's effects are not a mysterious pulling force... but are instead caused when objects with mass/energy distort the SHAPE of space-time fabric around them. *What does this really mean?*

*A planet in orbit around a star follows a curved trajectory not because of a "pull" of the star on the planet... but rather because space-time is warped in the vicinity of the star. This changes our entire view of what gravity actually is!*

Sun

*Tremendous Mass "Presses" on the Fabric of Space-time Drawing Planets into Orbit*

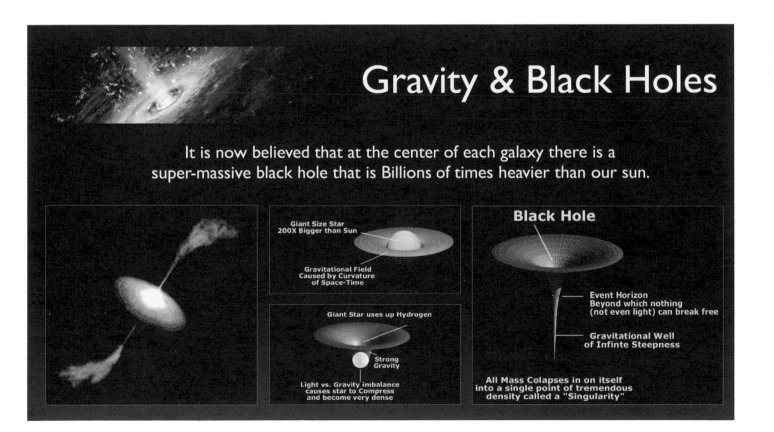

# Gravity & Black Holes

It is now believed that at the center of each galaxy there is a super-massive black hole that is Billions of times heavier than our sun.

**Giant Size Star 200X Bigger than Sun**

**Gravitational Field Caused by Curvature of Space-Time**

**Giant Star uses up Hydrogen**

**Strong Gravity**

**Light vs. Gravity imbalance causes star to Compress and become very dense**

**Black Hole**

**Event Horizon** Beyond which nothing (not even light) can break free

**Gravitational Well of Infinte Steepness**

**All Mass Colapses in on itself into a single point of tremendous density called a "Singularity"**

# 400 Billion Stars in Our Galaxy

*1 Light Year is 6 Trillion Miles*
*Orion's Belt is 1270 Light Years Away*

Our Solar System

Orion's Belt

*98,000 Light Years Across*

# "Galaxy Clusters"

Gravity Gives Galaxies the Natural Tendency to Clump Together

*Virgo Galaxy Cluster*
*40 Million Light Years Away*

*Abel Galaxy Super Cluster*
*2 Billion Light Years Away*

*The Galaxy clusters*
*are themselves clustered...*
*forming "Super-Clusters"*

# The Great Wall of Galaxies

◆ Stars and their orbiting Planets are organized into Galaxies, which in turn form clusters and superclusters that are separated by immense Voids.

◆ In 1989 Astronomers discovered an even larger structure they called "The Great Wall". It is a *sheet of galaxies* more than 500 million light years long and 200 Million Wide!

  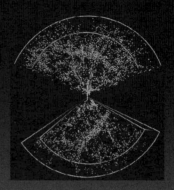

# Web of Galaxy Clusters

◆ This is a map of the first 1 billion light years of connecting Galaxy Superclusters near our Milkyway.

◆ NASA estimates there are atleast 400 billion galaxies in the known universe, which looks like a web.

◆ Astronomers can now see Galaxy Superclusters many billions of light years away. *Telescopes are now being made that can see planets orbiting around their parent stars.*

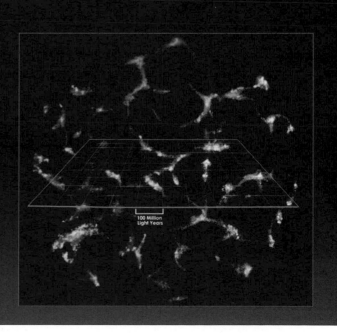

# Searching for Other Earths

NASA's first mission capable of finding Earth-size and smaller planets

Astronomer Alan Boss of the NASA Astrobiology Institute estimates that there are between 1-30 billion small rocky planets like Mars, Venus or Earth orbiting around a sun within our Milkyway Galaxy.

Milky Way Galaxy

◆ Since 2006, NASA's Kepler mission has begun the ginormus task of surveying over 100,00 stars. They are looking for terrestrial planets in the habitable zone the region around the parent star that is neither too hot or too cold for liquid water to exist.

*Dave Latham, at the Harvard-Smithsonian Center for Astrophysics said this about their current search: "Until recently, technology was only sensitive enough to pick up larger more massive planets than Earth, but improvements now make the discovery of a second Earth highly likely. It could happen almost any time now. We have the technological capability to identify Earth-like planets around the smallest stars even now."*

# History of Earth

◆ Modern Science says Earth formed 4.6 Billion Years ago and that 1 billion years later the first single celled organisms appeared.

◆ Dinosaurs bones have been discovered at excavation sites like this. Scientists believe dinosaurs first appeared 250 million years ago.

# Human Beings

◆ The oldest fossil evidence for anatomically modern humans is about 130,000 years old in Africa, and there is evidence for modern humans in Asia 90,000 years ago.

# Ancient People

Archeological evidence suggests "Modern Human Beings" learned more in the last 100,000 years than we may realize.

# They Perfectly Stacked 10 Ton Blocks

Modern Archeology claims:

The stones used in the construction of the Great Pyramid were cut, hauled, and placed by thousands of workers over a few generations.

Reality Shows: Several documented attempts fail to replicate (using pulley lever methods) what the early Egyptian builders achieved. *Even modern technology cannot duplicate the seamless, mortarless construction!*

# Modern Science Tried to Duplicate

In the 1970's, a Japanese team "well funded" by Nissan tried to build a 1/3$^{rd}$ scale model of the Great Pyramid *using the methods Archeologists claimed the ancient Egyptians used.*

The Result:

*Nissan's team could not duplicate a single step in the process; in fact, they couldn't duplicate any steps without modern machinery, and even that failed miserably!*

# Engineers are still Baffled in 2008

Inside the Kings Chamber of the Great Pyramid 43 granite blocks weighing 70 tons each were supposedly quarried with dolomite hammers, lifted out of the bedrock with pulleys and rope, and transported 500 miles down the river.

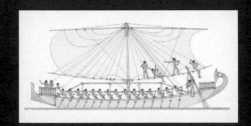

*Nissan's Egyptian-like boats all sank. So they called in a modern ferry to transport the blocks.*

*Once at the site... the heavy blocks could not be dragged over planks because they sank into the sand. They could not lift the blocks seamlessly into place... so they used a high tech crane!*

# The 400 Ton Obelisk

◆ Using stone hammers & fiber ropes Nissan came back and tried to raise a 35 ton obelisk...

◆ Modern Experiments backed by large amounts of money and manpower disprove the current theories that these wonders were built using tools 3500 BC. So how was it done?

*A man with a 4th Grade Education may shed some light into how it was possible...*

# Coral Castle and the
# 5 Foot Edward Leedskalnin

*with a 4th Grade Education*

◆ In 1920, Ed without any assistance or large machinery single handedly built the Coral Castle in Homestead, FL

◆ After it was first built, Ed decided he didn't like the property and moved single stones weighing over 30 tons about 20 minutes drive south.

*Ed published a series of books in which he argued forcefully that physicists did not understand electricity and were working from an incomplete picture of the true nature of the laws of magnetism.*

# Many blocks weighed 50 Tons... Ed was 95 pounds.

MAGNETIC
CURRENT

By
EDWARD LEEDSKALNIN
ROCK GATE
HOMESTEAD, FLORIDA
U. S. A.

◆ People have compared Ed's secret method of construction to Stonehenge and Pyramids

<u>Quote from Ed</u>: "North & South Pole Magnets are the 'Cosmic Force' and the building blocks of nature's perpetual transformation of matter. These magnetic currents pass through the Earth."

# Unexplainable Archeology

- Stonehenge is over 5000 years old.

- Many of the stones weigh 40 tons.

- Some are buried 8 ft under ground.

# What does it all mean?

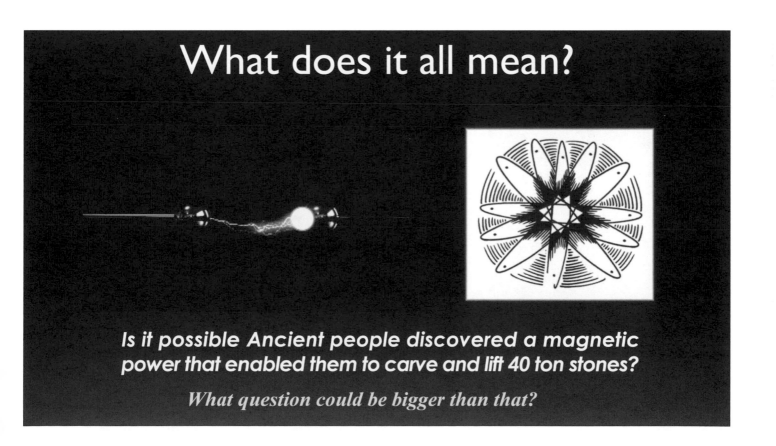

*Is it possible Ancient people discovered a magnetic power that enabled them to carve and lift 40 ton stones?*

*What question could be bigger than that?*

# The Future of the Human Race

*What are some of the BIGGEST Challenges we face?*

# Clean the Earth

Fact #1:  Even if we cleaned the Earth of all the Pollution...
People would still fight over who gets the best land...
the most resources... just as we've done for 6000 years

# Separation Consciousness

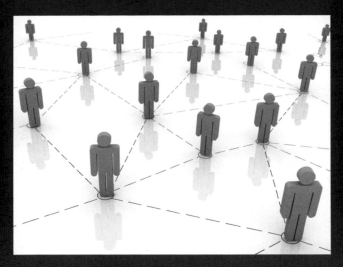

Fact #2: Most of the World sees itself as "separate" from other people outside of their immediate family.

# Changing Our Reality

*Us vs. Them Consciousness is no longer working*

Fact #3: Since the Great Flood... man has fought war after war.
*When will all the hatred & bitterness end?*

# If we can't Forgive each other how can we expect entire nations to?

Fact #4: All people in the Entire Universe of 400 Billion Galaxies originate from the One True Source.

# ALL IS ONE

*We believe that when Humanity realizes its connection with ALL of life... World Peace is possible.*

# Transforming Our View on Disease

Our organs and cells exist as one entity.
Why should we separate diseases - rather then nurture our whole body?

# Qi is a Unifying Agent

Qigong is the fastest way to FEEL the Non-Physical Spiritual Energy.

*Because its so powerful in large groups... it can lead to widespread Unity Consciousness as Billions suddenly "Experience Their Oneness"*

# Our Vision

## The Ultimate All is One Experience

# Photo Montage of Supreme Science Events

# Ft. Lauderdale Convention Center
## November 12th-15th, 2005

# Ft. Lauderdale Convention Center
## January 7th-10th, 2006

# Tampa Convention Center
## March 4th-7th, 2006

# Qigong Mountain Retreat  *Blueridge, Georgia
## April 27th-May1st , 2006

# Atlanta Metropolitan Club
## May 20th-23rd, 2006

# Orlando Convention Center
## June 10th-13th, 2006

# Qigong Mountain Retreat  *Blueridge, Georgia
## August 4th-8th, 2006

# College of Santa Fe
## August 19th-22nd, 2006

# Ft. Lauderdale Convention Center
## November 18th-21st, 2006

# Asheville Civic Center
## February 24th-27th, 2007

# Tampa Bay India Cultural Center
## March 24th-27th, 2007

# Qigong Mountain Retreat  *Kauai, Hawaii
## April 20th-27th , 2007

# University of Colorado Boulder
## June 2nd-5th, 2007

# University of Maryland
## June 16th-19th, 2007

# Austin Convention Center
## June 30th-July 3rd, 2007

# University of California, San Diego
## August 11th-14th, 2007

# University of California, Los Angeles
## August 18th-21st, 2007

# University of California, Berkeley
## August 25th-28th, 2007

# Advanced Qigong Facilitator Training (2nd Annual)
## November 10th-13th, 2007
## February 1st– 5th, 2008

# Chattanooga Convention Center, Tennessee
## March 1st-4th, 2008

# Wim Hof: Miami Beach, FL
## Tumo Internal Heat Generation Seminar
## May 2nd-6th, 2008

We turned the air conditioner full blast over night.
Wim taught us his Pranayama method to increase heat .

His technique was strikingly similar to
9-Breath Method, but with key unique points.

Jeff on Day 5 taking an Ice Bath for 12 minutes.
Nobody talks when they get in... its right to the technique.

Norwood, Dianne & Rebecca doing
TUMO Inside a restaurant freezer at minus 20 F.

# Orlando Convention Center *1800 People!*
## June 28th-July 1st, 2008

# University of Maryland
## July 19th-22nd, 2008

# Advanced Qigong Facilitator Training (3rd Annual)
## October 3rd-7th, 2008
## January 23rd-26th, 2009

# Ft. Lauderdale Courtyard Marriott
## November 22nd-25th, 2008

# Atlanta Georgia World Congress Convention Center
## February 28th—March 3rd, 2009

# Orlando Convention Center   *2000 People!*
## April 25th-28th, 2009

# Orlando Convention Center  *2000 People!*
## April 25th-28th, 2009

# Advanced Food Healing Workshop
## May 22nd & 23rd, 2009

# Tampa India Cultural Center
## July 11th-14th, 2009

# Advanced Qigong Facilitator Training *(4th Annual)*
## August 8th-12th, 2009

# Advanced Qigong 9-Breath Healing
## August 13th-14th, 2009

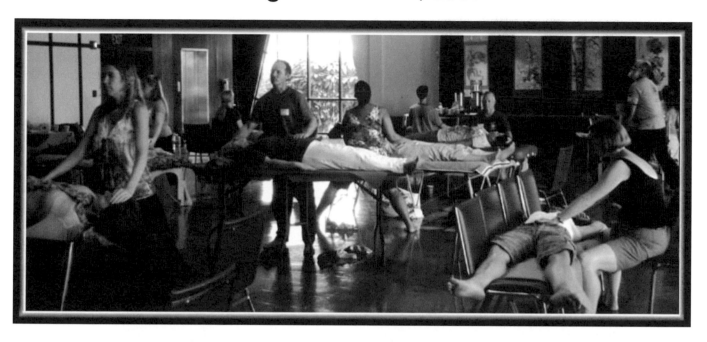

# Level-3 Advanced Qigong Facilitator Training (4th Annual)
## November 6th-9th, 2009

# Wuji for Kids
## November 7th-8th, 2009

# Miami Beach Convention Center
## November 14th-17th, 2009

# Chicago McCormick Place
## March 6th-9th, 2010

# Georgia World Congress Center
## March 27th-30th, 2010

# Artwork Created
# Under the Influence of Qi

Dodecahedron 1998

Flower of Life 1999

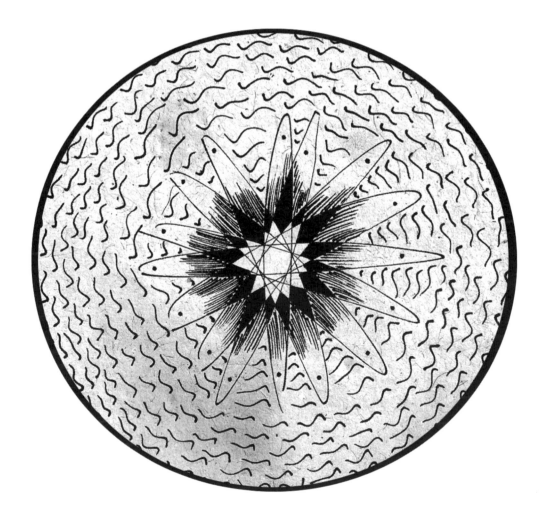

Vibrations from Source 1999

Star of Truth 2000  (3ft on Ceiling)

Qi Flower 2000

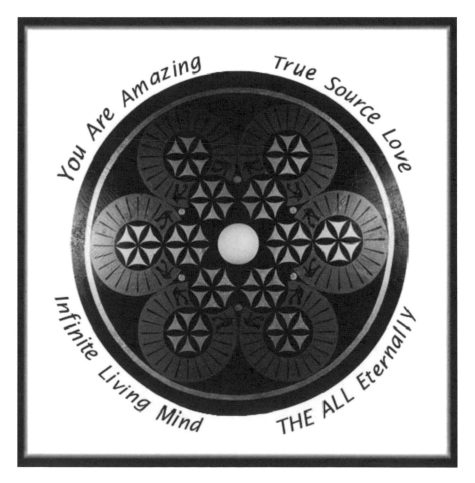

Embryo 2001  (5ft on Ceiling)

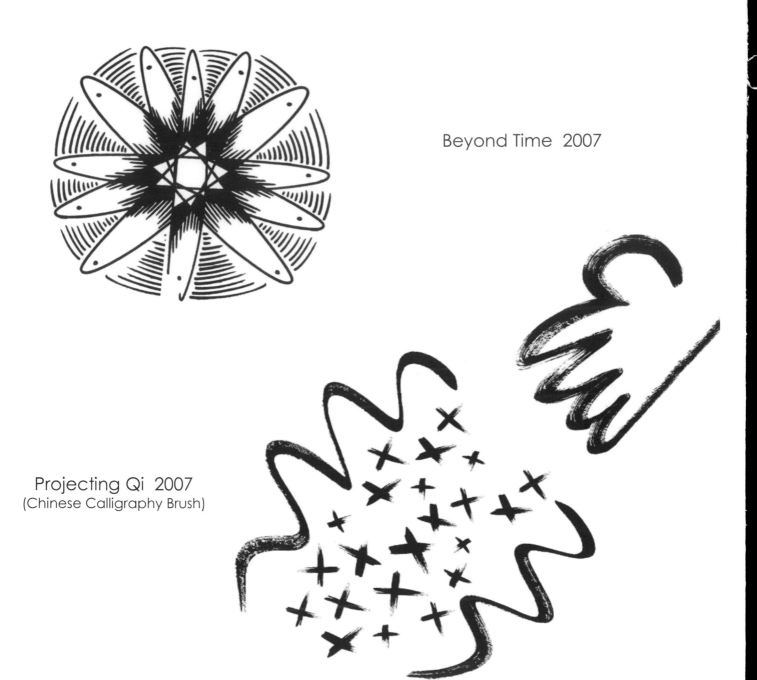

Beyond Time 2007

Projecting Qi 2007
(Chinese Calligraphy Brush)

Resonating Fields 2008

Qi Love 2007 (Chinese Calligraphy Brush)

Intelligence 2008 (4ft on Ceiling)

New Energy  2010  (Notepad Doodle During Instructor Exam)

Fruit of Life 2010 (3ft on Ceiling Above Bed)

Metatron  (Computer Connects Every Center)

# The Future of the Human Race

May God Bless our children, the inheritors of the New Earth. For there is no human experience that goes beyond parenthood for seeing the true nature of man. My son is named Trew, for that he is. When he was 2 years old he was actively speaking and one day he got upset because I laughed at him. His feelings were hurt and even at the innocent age of 2, he knew that I had laughed at his own expense. He said, "What are you laughing at!" and huffed off. I followed him and gently touched his shoulder, "I am sorry Trew. Please forgive me." Trew replied, "Yeah... ok." I was sad now. "Trew! I love you. You are God's creation and you are made by his hands. You are perfect. Do you forgive me?" I'll never forget when that 2 year old looked me locked square in the eyes and with the nobility of a king and said, "Of course, Daddy. I always forgive you. Never forget that. Don't you always know. I always forgive you." The seriousness in which he spoke told me that his higher self was teaching me. Since that time Trew has taught me Love on levels I never knew possible. It is my son Trew that drives me onward. For the children are the future. We must offer them a brighter future with a clean environment and peace-loving people.

# LOOK FOR BESTSELLING QIGONG & FOOD-HEALING DVDS, BOOKS AND LIVE TRAINING SEMINARS

## WWW.QIGONG.COM
## (800)-298-8970

**AWARD WINNING ANIMATED QIGONG VIDEOS**

**NINE-BREATH METHOD & BREATH EMPOWERMENT**

**FOOD-BASED HEALING CONQUERING ANY DISEASE**